W9-BTE-817

EYE ON
Art

ROMANTICISM

by Stuart A. Kallen

LUCENT BOOKS
An imprint of Thomson Gale, a part of The Thomson Corporation

THOMSON
✦
GALE
™

Detroit • New York • San Francisco • New Haven, Conn. • Waterville, Maine • London

THOMSON

GALE

© 2007 Thomson Gale, a part of The Thomson Corporation.

Thomson and Star Logo are trademarks and Gale and Lucent Books are registered trademarks used herein under license.

For more information, contact
Lucent Books
27500 Drake Rd.
Farmington Hills, MI 48331-3535
Or you can visit our Internet site at http://www.gale.com

LIBRARY OF CONGRESS CATALOGING-IN-PUBLICATION DATA

Kallen, Stuart A., 1955–
Romanticism / by Stuart A. Kallen.
    p. cm. — (Eye on art)
Includes bibliographical references.
ISBN-13: 978-1-59018-962-7 (hardcover : alk. paper)
ISBN-10: 1-59018-962-0 (hardcover : alk. paper)
1. Romanticism in art—Juvenile literature. I. Title.
NX454.5.R6K35 2007
709.03'42—dc22

2006018682

Printed in the United States of America

CONTENTS

Foreword

"Art has no other purpose than to brush aside . . . everything that veils reality from us in order to bring us face to face with reality itself."

—French philosopher Henri-Louis Bergson

Some thirty-one thousand years ago, early humans painted strikingly sophisticated images of horses, bison, rhinoceroses, bears, and other animals on the walls of a cave in southern France. The meaning of these elaborate pictures is unknown, although some experts speculate that they held ceremonial significance. Regardless of their intended purpose, the Chauvet-Pont-d'Arc cave paintings represent some of the first known expressions of the artistic impulse.

From the Paleolithic era to the present day, human beings have continued to create works of visual art. Artists have developed painting, drawing, sculpture, engraving, and many other techniques to produce visual representations of landscapes, the human form, religious and historical events, and countless other subjects. The artistic impulse also finds expression in glass, jewelry, and new forms inspired by new technology. Indeed, judging by humanity's prolific artistic output throughout history, one must conclude that the compulsion to produce art is an inherent aspect of being human, and the results are among humanity's greatest cultural achievements: masterpieces such as the architectural marvels of ancient Greece, Michelangelo's perfectly rendered statue *David*, Vincent van Gogh's visionary painting *Starry Night*, and endless other treasures.

The creative impulse serves many purposes for society. At its most basic level, art is a form of entertainment or the means for a satisfying or pleasant aesthetic experience. But art's true power lies not in its potential to entertain and delight but in its ability to enlighten, to reveal the truth, and by doing so to uplift the human spirit and transform the human race.

One of the primary functions of art has been to serve religion. For most of Western history, for example, artists were paid by the church to produce works with religious themes and subjects. Art was thus a tool to help human beings transcend mundane, secular reality and achieve spiritual enlightenment. One of the best-known, and largest-scale, examples of Christian religious art is the Sistine Chapel in the Vatican in Rome. In 1508 Pope Julius II commissioned Italian Renaissance artist Michelangelo to paint the chapel's vaulted ceiling, an area of 640 square yards (535 sq. m). Michelangelo spent four years on scaffolding, his neck craned, creating a panoramic fresco of some three hundred human figures. His paintings depict Old Testament prophets and heroes, sibyls of Greek mythology, and nine scenes from the Book of Genesis, including the Creation of Adam, the Fall of Adam and Eve from the Garden of Eden, and the Flood. The ceiling of the Sistine Chapel is considered one of the greatest works of Western art and has inspired the awe of countless Christian pilgrims and other religious seekers. As eighteenth-century German poet and author Johann Wolfgang von Goethe wrote, "Until you have seen this Sistine Chapel, you can have no adequate conception of what man is capable of."

In addition to inspiring religious fervor, art can serve as a force for social change. Artists are among the visionaries of any culture. As such, they often perceive injustice and wrongdoing and confront others by reflecting what they see in their work. One classic example of art as social commentary was created in May 1937, during the brutal Spanish civil war. On May 1 Spanish artist Pablo Picasso learned of the recent attack on the small Basque village of Guernica by German airplanes allied with fascist forces led by Francisco Franco. The German pilots had used the village for target practice, a three-hour bombing that killed sixteen hundred civilians. Picasso, living in Paris, channeled his outrage over the massacre into his painting *Guernica,* a black, white, and gray mural that depicts dismembered animals and fractured human figures whose faces are contorted in agonized expressions. Initially, critics and the public condemned the painting as an incoherent hodgepodge, but the work soon came to be seen as a powerful antiwar statement and remains an iconic symbol of the violence and terror that dominated world events during the remainder of the twentieth century.

The impulse to create art—whether painting animals with crude pigments on a cave wall, sculpting a human form from marble, or commemorating human tragedy in a mural—thus serves many purposes. It offers an entertaining diversion, nourishes the imagination and the spirit, decorates and beautifies the world, and chronicles the age. But underlying all these functions is the desire to reveal that which is obscure—to illuminate, clarify, and perhaps ennoble. As Picasso himself stated, "The purpose of art is washing the dust of daily life off our souls."

The Eye on Art series is intended to assist readers in understanding the various roles of art in society. Each volume offers an in-depth exploration of a major artistic movement, medium, figure, or profession. All books in the series are beautifully illustrated with full-color photographs and diagrams. Riveting narrative, clear technical explanation, informative sidebars, fully documented quotes, a bibliography, and a thorough index all provide excellent starting points for research and discussion. With these features, the Eye on Art series is a useful introduction to the world of art—a world that can offer both insight and inspiration.

Introduction

An Artistic Movement

In the world of art, the most creative and talented people are seldom satisfied to follow rules laid down by previous generations. In almost every period in history, brash young artists have sought to break traditions concerning color, perspective, subject matter, and acceptable content. Often artists did so at their peril, and some artists later recognized as masters faced harsh criticism in their own time. A few died in poverty because they cast aside cherished customs and practices. This was especially true in the late eighteenth century for the artists, poets, writers, and musical composers of what came to be called the Romantic movement.

Romantic painters, whose emotional work inspired feelings of awe, foreboding, dreamlike wonder, horror, and fear, were rebelling against artistic rules that were deeply entrenched in society. These traditions were based on the intellectual movement known as the Enlightenment, which developed in the early seventeenth century. Prominent Enlightenment philosophers valued rational thought and the stoic philosophy of the ancient Greeks, which stated that art, music, and literature should be free from undue passion.

When innovative painters produced startlingly dramatic and emotional artwork, Enlightenment thinkers responded

Moses and the Burning Bush by William Blake is a romantic painting meant to inspire feelings of awe and dreamlike wonder.

by calling them romantics. This was considered a derogatory term and was largely used at the time to describe someone who was either an impractical dreamer or a hopelessly love-struck youth. A few artists rejected the term; others embraced it and gave it new meaning. In their works they created contrasting worlds of fantasy and horror, love and hatred, faith and skepticism, and the beauty of nature amid the hell of warfare. And in doing so, romantic artists fundamentally changed the way people thought about their own lives, their innermost feelings, and the often turbulent world around them.

Passions, Individualism, and Imagination

Artists associated with this new state of mind came primarily from northern Europe—present-day Germany, France, and Great Britain—and the United States. They include Caspar David Friedrich, Théodore Géricault, Eugène Delacroix, William Blake, Joseph Mallord William Turner, Thomas Cole, and hundreds of others. With bold brushwork these painters created richly colored, dramatic art that exalted human passions, individualism, and imagination.

Romantic artists also idealized nature, landscapes, and the wilderness at a time when the countryside of North America and western Europe was quickly filling with farms, canals, roads, railways, and industrial pollution. To capture the natural world beyond Western civilization, some artists traveled to what were considered exotic locales, such as Tahiti, Africa, and the American West. In these places they recorded the cultures of indigenous peoples in an idealized fashion, conceiving them as uncorrupted by modern civilization.

Most important, romantic art was born during an era of revolution in America and France and at a time when wars were an ongoing fact of life in continental Europe. These conditions inspired artists to depict the heroics and horrors of battle and revolution in a startlingly realistic manner that was unique at the time.

"New Worlds of Information and Emotion"

During the age of romantic art, most people did not travel far beyond their hometowns. Although wars, revolutions, and exotic locales were described in books, the only visual images of these things came from paintings. (Photography did not come into widespread use until the 1850s.) Therefore, as Frederick Cummings explains in *Romantic Art in Britain*, people relied on painters to interpret events:

> Compared with our experiences, the intellectual and emotional contexts of a country squire or a London scholar in 1760 were limited. Today, we easily accept numerous concurrent levels of sensation. Mass communications and streamlined travel have caused the interweaving of many formerly isolated worlds, each with its own character and rationale. The cultural experience of the eighteenth-century man was restricted to literature, to the music and works of art available in his

Romantic landscape paintings, such as Thomas Cole's *View of Monte Video*, idealized nature at a time of increasing industrialization and settlement.

country house or in the London exhibitions or theatres, and to rare travel on the continent. Paintings, drawings, and prints were to become the particular visual arts which made it possible for the eighteenth-century individual to enter vicariously into new worlds of information and emotion. Much of the information gathered was either visual or immediately translated into visual form. As a result, the [romantic] artists were among the first to grasp the popular implication of a series of new areas of experience which then found their first and most complete expression and their widest distribution through the visual arts.[1]

Since this expression of experience was considered so important to society as a whole, great debates erupted over the content of romantic paintings. This attention often produced great public interest in romanticism, which fueled the growth of the style. As a result, creative people during the romantic era produced an abundance of immortal paintings, plays, poems, and novels in a relatively short time span. Some of these works were valued in their time; others were not appreciated by society until long after their creators were dead. Whatever the case, romantic artists guaranteed their place in history by being among the first painters to express their personal feelings passionately on canvas. This revolution in self-expression laid the groundwork for later artistic styles such as realism, surrealism, and modern expressionism.

Today, the kinds of stunning artistic visions of color, light, and drama developed by romantic painters are a part of everyday life. They are seen in galleries, photographs, movies such as *The Lord of the Rings*, and even comic books. And the romantic influence in the art world remains strong—today painters are expected to communicate their emotions, dreams, and opinions through art. Those who take this artistic freedom for granted owe a debt of gratitude to a group of visionaries who worked from about 1760 to the late 1800s and whose paintings are as important and inspirational today as they were when they were created.

Romance and Revolution

Romanticism is a label applied to bold, dramatic, and emotional works of art, literature, and music produced in the late 1700s and throughout the 1800s. Those who took part in the romantic movement thought of themselves not simply as artists but as revolutionaries who were breaking with established artistic and social rules. Romantics exalted individualism over conformity, imagination over reason, and passionate emotions above rational thought. Along with accepted sentiments such as love, tranquility, and triumph, they portrayed rarely depicted emotions such as revulsion, horror, and hatred. Whatever the subject, the romantics expressed the extremities of the human condition in a confrontational manner meant to shock conventional society.

Romantic artists did not create their paintings simply to express raw emotions or gain public attention, however. Their objective was to free their emotions and allow their imaginations to soar, by using a creative process that would, in turn, allow them to make the most of their ultimate artistic powers and, beyond art, could help them become perfect beings, or even gods. In this perfect state of existence, the romantic could finally come to understand and reconcile the opposing forces in the world, both the positive and the negative—natural beauty and war, health and sickness, happiness and death.

A Revolutionary Concept

The articulation of extreme emotions in art was considered revolutionary in the late 1700s, due to the social and artistic conventions of the era, known as the Age of Enlightenment. It was a time when elite intellectuals and philosophers saw themselves boldly leading the human race toward progress based on rational thought, ethics, and democracy. These beliefs stood in opposition to powerful royal and religious leaders who ruled by tyranny and exploited people's fears and superstitions.

The theories behind the Age of Enlightenment were the basis for both the American and French revolutions, as well as revolutionary movements in Latin America and Poland. While the romantics also considered themselves revolutionaries, they did not accept the basic philosophies of the Enlightenment, nor did they support the beliefs of those who ruled church or state.

Intellectuals of the Enlightenment believed that human beings could embrace perfection and create an earthly utopia. These philosophers hoped to emulate the democratic society formed around the eighth century B.C. in ancient Greece, which they saw as a model of human excellence. As Lorenz Eitner writes in *Neoclassicism and Romanticism*,

> Antiquity provided the example of a state of humanity so exalted that a future worth striving for could be conceived in its image. This gave the movement of progress a concrete goal, and . . . a practical method for reaching it: the systematic study of and imitation of Antiquity, that historical moment of human perfection which, having once before been realized, could be attained again.[2]

The Most Perfect Beauty

In the world of art, the Enlightenment passion for classical Greece was seen in the popular style called neoclassicism.

Artists who worked in the neoclassical discipline based their artwork on ancient Greek sculptures. These statues, which often depicted gods in dramatic poses based on Greek mythology, were said to epitomize the perfect ideals of human beauty. The facial expressions depicted on the Greek gods were often stoic and calm— they did not show strong emotions. For example, a well-known ancient statue showed the Greek mythological character Laocoön being crushed by serpents, and although a human being would experience intense pain during such an ordeal, the facial expression of the figure is sedate and tranquil.

Writing about this statue in 1755, Prussian art critic Johann Joachim Winckelmann initiated a heated debate about the emotional content of art. Winckelmann believed that artists should create only beautiful art and avoid the depiction of strong human emotions. Winckelmann objected to any portrayal of Laocoön, for example, as grimacing, wincing, or screaming out in horror.

Voltaire was a leading proponent of the Enlightenment philosophy in France.

Winckelmann was an extremely influential critic and his beliefs were widely supported by other critics and by artists themselves. In 1772, for example, the famous painter Sir Joshua Reynolds told art students at the Royal Academy of London, "If you mean to preserve the most perfect beauty in *its most perfect state*, you cannot express the passions, all of which produce distortion and deformity, more or less, in the most beautiful faces." For those who felt restricted by his words, Reynolds added, "We need not be mortified or discouraged at not being able to execute the conceptions of a romantic imagination. Art has its boundaries, though imagination has none."[3]

JOHANN WINCKELMANN AND NEOCLASSICISM

Neoclassicism is the name given to the art period that preceded romanticism. It was so named because Enlightenment thinkers incorporated artistic, literary, architectural, and philosophical values from the era of classical Greek culture, which flourished between 700 and 300 B.C. (*Neo-* means "new.")

In the world of visual arts, Prussian author and art critic Johann Joachim Winckelmann (1717–1768) was one of the most influential neo-classicist thinkers. In 1755, he moved to Rome, where he studied art created in ancient Egypt, Greece, and Italy. Upon returning home in 1764, Winckelmann wrote his *History of Ancient Art*, which influenced a generation of French and English art students to emulate the art of classical Greece, thus creating the neoclassical style.

Winckelmann believed that beauty should not be expressed in passionate terms but in what he described as noble simplicity and quiet grandeur. In painting, he thought, colors should be muted and delicately rendered so they did not distract from the beauty of the subject. Although neoclassical artists agreed with Winckelmann's opinions, he set off a rebellion among artists who wanted to incorporate extreme emotion, color, and drama into their work. These artists later came to be called romantics.

Neoclassical paintings such as this one were intended to depict human beauty at its most perfect.

Reynolds's choice of the word *romantic* to describe limitless imagination and free expression was no accident. He was alluding to artists whose work, at the time, was considered wild, fantastic, and extreme. Winckelmann was another critic of such paintings, writing that the figures were portrayed in "contortions and strange postures," "[with] froth and bombast," and "violent passions."[4]

New and Old Attitudes

The emotions seen in romantic art were shocking to Enlightenment critics because romanticism was more than simply an artistic or literary movement. According to Petra ten-Doesschate Chu, writing in *Nineteenth Century Art*, romanticism was

> a state of mind, a new attitude to the world that differed radically from Enlightenment rationalism. In short, Romanticism [valued] emotions, faith, and spirituality over intellect and reason. Romantics preferred spontaneity to calculation, individuality over conformity, and the freedom of nature over the constraints of culture.[5]

Although the beliefs of the romantics were considered new and different, they were based on ideas that had been circulating for centuries. One such concept was characterized by the word *sublime*, which was used to define works that were so astounding that they could evoke feelings of the mystical or supernatural in the viewer.

The romantics' beliefs about the sublime were adapted from the treatise *On the Sublime* by first-century A.D. Greek author Longinus. As British art historian William Vaughn writes in *Romanticism and Art*, Longinus "recognized that [artistic] pleasure could be stimulated not only by the awareness of beauty, but also by a more mysterious and elating experience known as the 'Sublime'. . . an overpowering form of beauty . . . which saw the ultimate perfection of earthly forms in Heaven . . . [and provided humans] with the closest experience of the Divine."[6]

Romantic thinkers reduced this complicated concept to a simplified form: The sublime was seen as rooted in the two most basic—and powerful—human emotions, love and hate. According to philosopher Edmund Burke, love was expressed as attraction while hate was expressed as repulsion. As Vaughn writes,

> While a sense of beauty was aroused by those objects that seemed attractive, a sense of sublimity was induced by those objects whose properties seemed repellent. . . . Burke's theory was vital to the Romantics both because it emphasized the suggestive quality of art and because it gave new importance to the disturbing. The artist who concentrated on [painting repellent images to evoke emotional feelings] now was not simply engineering a . . . thrill; he had become an explorer.[7]

Heroes and Monsters

Longinus's writings were one source of inspiration for the romantics. Another—and the one that gave the romantic movement its name—was found in episodic stories written between the twelfth and early fifteenth centuries. Writers in this medieval period produced dramatic tales of love, hate, horror, and death. These stories were called romances by fourteenth-century English author Geoffrey Chaucer because they were written in the Romance languages—French, Italian, and Spanish—that developed from the Latin of the Roman Empire.

Most medieval romances were based on a central heroic figure. The most popular tales concerned the mighty deeds of three men—Alexander the Great, king of Macedonia in the fourth century B.C., French king Charlemagne, in the eighth century A.D., and the mythological English King Arthur. The stories of these men were known as tales of chivalry because they emphasized the idealized heroic qualities of knighthood, such as bravery, courtesy, honor, and gallantry toward women. In some romances, the heroes worked with wizards who used magic to fight supernatural villains, horrific evil spirits, repulsive witches, and soul-snatching demons.

During the romantic era, the medieval romances inspired writers to incorporate disturbing concepts of horror into their literature. Such elements were described as Gothic, a term that alluded to a form of medieval architecture, and as a result, became a synonym for *medieval*. One of the most famous authors to make use of Gothic devices was the German Johann Wolfgang von Goethe, whose 1806 story *Faust* told of a man who sold his soul to the devil in trade for immortality and the love of an otherwise unattainable woman.

Another classic Gothic horror tale of the romantic era, *Frankenstein, or the Modern Prometheus*, was written by Mary Shelley. This 1818 novel tells of a doctor who builds a monster from body parts stolen from corpses and brings it to life through medieval magic.

English author Geoffrey Chaucer used the term "romance" in the fourteenth century to describe stories about the heroic deeds of great men.

Images of Death

Shelley and Goethe were not the only writers to incorporate gloomy elements into their works. Poets such as Percy Bysshe Shelley, Samuel Taylor Coleridge, and William Wordsworth often wrote melancholy verses about ancient ruins, castles, and abbeys—macabre remnants of real Gothic culture. Romantic painters, in turn, adopted these dreary images to evoke notions of haunted lost worlds and glum thoughts of death and decay. Other widely used morbid romantic images were crows, gnarled trees, disinterred coffins, grave markers, and funeral processions. The use of these symbols in the paintings of Caspar David Friedrich is discussed by Raffaella Russo in *Friedrich*:

> The crows flying slowly around the [dead] oak tree are the dark harbingers of death. . . . The portals of ruined

abbeys become a symbol of death, the gates to the eternal life beyond. Life on earth is no more than waiting for death, since only death can give meaning to life. The wizened branches of the trees, the dead leaves, and the steep slopes are not only symbols of the transitory nature of life, but also of the hope that death will mark the transition from life on earth to life in heaven.[8]

Comparable symbols may be found in other common romantic images such as foggy mountains, foreboding clouds, and seashores littered with wrecked ships.

Reacting to War and Revolution

The most obvious allusions to horror found in romantic paintings were battlefields littered with dead bodies. These were taken not from ancient tales but from the wars and revolutions that were parts of everyday life. During that era, Europe was ruled by despotic kings who governed with absolute dictatorial powers that they believed were granted to them by God. While average citizens watched in fascination and horror, competing European monarchs launched war after war. England, France, Austria, and Spain continually fought over colonial possessions in North and South America and clashed over who would sit on the thrones of Europe. This jostling for power resulted in long, bloody conflicts that raged across the European continent throughout the eighteenth century.

The French Revolution, which began in 1789, was perhaps the most inspirational and controversial to romantic artists. While many of them

Mary Shelley's *Frankenstein, or the Modern Prometheus*, published in 1818, is one of the most popular Gothic horror stories from the romantic era.

ROMANTIC POETRY

Percy Bysshe Shelley was one of the most renowned of the romantic poets. His poems such as "Ode to the West Wind," "Ozymandias," and "Alastor, or The Spirit of Solitude," often evoked melancholy images of nature that were an inspiration to romantic painters. Such imagery is rife in Shelley's 1817 poem, "Mont Blanc," written in the Swiss Alps:

> Some say that gleams of a remoter world
> Visit the soul in sleep, that death is slumber,
> And that its shapes the busy thoughts outnumber
> Of those who wake and live.—I look on high;
> Has some unknown omnipotence unfurled
> The veil of life and death? or do I lie
> In dream, and does the mightier world of sleep
> Spread far around and inaccessibly
> Its circles? For the very spirit falls,
> Driven like a homeless cloud
>   from steep to steep
> That vanishes among the
>   viewless gales!
> Far, far above, piercing the
>   infinite sky,
> Mont Blanc appears—still,
>   snowy, and serene…

Some romantic painters found inspiration in the works of poets such as Percy Bysshe Shelley.

Quoted in Hugh Honour, *Romanticism*. New York: Harper and Row, 1979, p. 315.

embraced the ideals of individual freedom and democracy promoted by French revolutionaries, the revolution itself resulted in the deaths of tens of thousands of innocent citizens. In addition, once the French monarchy was overthrown, the revolution's leaders waged a series of unsuccessful wars against Great Britain, Holland, and Spain that resulted in widespread misery. The ultimate failure of the revolutionaries resulted in Napoleon Bonaparte taking control of France in 1799. He, in turn, conquered most of Europe, throwing the continent into chaos until he was defeated in 1815.

These cataclysmic current events were impossible for romantics to ignore. Vaughn examines the artistic responses to the troubled times:

> At a time when the destiny of Europe hung in the balance, what was the creative genius to do? Should he enter the fray, creating propagandist proclamations for the faction he supported? Or should he remain aloof and provide an art whose nobility was an inspiration to man without dictating individual acts? Should he treat his contemporaries to the benefit of his own prophetic insights? Or should he use his perception to puncture pretence and draw attention to the basic human problems that the current conflicts involved? All these attitudes can be found among artists in Europe during the 1700s. Among . . . [the most remarkable] were those two great artists who developed prophetic and critical forms of independent commentary that were new to art: William Blake in England and Francisco de Goya in Spain.[9]

Goya's Unflinching Eye

As an Englishman, Blake was largely removed from the conflicts and revolutions taking place on the European continent. Goya, however, was an eyewitness to war. In addition, he suffered from a variety of physical and mental ailments that alienated him from society. Affected not only by the horrors of war he saw around him but also by his own demons and nightmares, Goya came to epitomize the quintessentially depressed and haunted romantic painter.

In 1792, when Goya was only forty-six, he went totally deaf in a short period of time after contracting a high fever. The artist was devastated by this turn of events. According to art historian Kenneth Clark in *The Romantic Rebellion*, "This man who had been in the thick of life was suddenly cut off from it. For some reason, human beings without their voices became for him grotesque and revolting and the solitude of his deafness was invaded by horrible monsters."[10]

In his isolation, Goya immersed himself in books about philosophy, culture, politics, and the French Revolution. Working in his studio, the artist created cartoon-like etchings that he said exposed the religious ignorance, folly, and superstitions that permeated society. In a series of eighty images published in 1799 as *Los Caprichos* (*The Caprices*), Goya turned an unflinching and satirical eye on Spanish society, the clergy, and the royal regime.

The first half of *Caprichos* focuses on the casual cruelties of everyday life. For example, the etching called *But He Broke the Pitcher* shows a mother, her face twisted in a spiteful expression, beating her child's exposed buttocks. The second set of etchings in *Caprichos* contains supernatural, romantic images that depict a world haunted by nightmarish demons. The picture titled *The Dream of Reason Produces Monsters*, for example, is a self-portrait of the artist asleep with his head down on a table. Goya's dreams, shown as owls and bats flying about the room, represent his intense dread, terror, and distress. The caption beneath the print explains the drawing: "Imagination abandoned by reason produces impossible monsters."[11]

In *The Dream of Reason Produces Monsters,* Francisco de Goya depicted himself as haunted by nightmares populated with demons and other terrors.

As an independent artist, Goya printed and sold the etchings himself. In an advertisement in Madrid's main newspaper, the artist makes clear the social commentary contained in his work:

> Since the artist is convinced that the censure of human errors and vice . . . may also be the object of Painting, he has chosen as subjects adequate for his work, from the multitude of follies and blunders common in every civil society, as well as from the vulgar prejudices and lies authorized by custom, ignorance or interest, those that he has thought most suitable matter for ridicule.[12]

Unlike many romantic paintings that portrayed wartime scenes in a heroic fashion, Francisco de Goya's *Execution of the Rebels on the Third of May* graphically depicted the horrors of human conflict.

Disasters of War

Although *Caprichos* was not a financial success, Goya continued to expose what he perceived as ignorance, violence, and hatred. His second series of etchings, *Disasters of War*, was

based upon the current events of that time. Between 1808 and 1814, Spain was brutally ruled by France, while Spanish loyalists fought the occupation. Goya did not take sides in the conflict, but he recorded the rapes, murders, and countless gory atrocities committed by both factions. One of the most visceral of the etchings, sarcastically titled *Great Heroism! Against Dead Men!*, shows three corpses, mutilated and castrated, with the head of one man impaled on a broken tree branch while his severed arms swing from a rope.

Fearing that the eighty-two plates of *Disasters of War* depicted the bestial nature of humankind too explicitly for public consumption, Goya never put the series on sale. The prints were finally published in 1863, thirty-five years after the artist's death.

Even as he was laboring over his etchings, Goya continued to express his feelings on monumental canvases. One of his most renowned paintings, *Execution of the Rebels on the Third of May*, depicts the massacre of rebellious civilians by French soldiers in 1808. Chu describes the scene and its symbolism:

> [We] see a group of captured rebels, led under cover of night to an execution ground where a French firing squad shoots them one by one. The powerful contrast between the soldiers and the rebels brings the dramatic scene to life. The soldiers, seen from the back, resemble automatons with their identical uniforms and poses. The rebels, lit by the lamp, show their humanity, mortality, and courage in the face of death. The man about to executed shows a dramatic range of emotions. Dressed in a white shirt and light pants, kneeling before his captors, he raises up his arms in a gesture both desperate and defiant. . . . The *Execution of the Rebels* is unprecedented in the history of painting, since it represents neither a glorious victory nor a heroic battle. Instead it portrays human slaughter in all its sordidness.[13]

Although Goya's images are harsh and forlorn, the positive aspect of Gothic heroism is also revealed. Commenting on *The*

Third of May, the artist stated that he was attempting to "perpetuate by the means of his brush the most notable and heroic actions of our glorious insurrection against the Tyrant of Europe [Napoleon]."[14] Goya continued to paint horrific images throughout his career. Some consider a series of paintings he made in 1819, nine years before his death, among the gloomiest and most hallucinogenic of the romantic era. Called the Black Paintings, these works were painted directly onto the walls of the artist's two-story home and never meant for public viewing. Removed to museums after Goya's death, the paintings show giant monsters battling in a mountain landscape, rituals of medieval witchcraft, and ghoulish characters in a variety of poses. The most shockingly savage of the Black Paintings, *Saturn Devouring His Son*, depicts the Greek myth of the god Saturn eating one of his own babies because he fears that one of his sons will someday overthrow him. Chu comments on the painting:

> In Goya's image, Saturn emerges from the dark, his face distorted with hatred and fear. His mouth opens wide to take another bite from a human. . . . Saturn devouring his own children represents Goya's conclusion that mankind is ultimately self-destructive, for to kill one's offspring is to destroy the future.[15]

Finding Peace in Landscapes

Not all paintings from the romantic era depict scenes of supernatural horror, mass murder, or cannibalism. Many painters created landscapes of mountains, fields, and forests. These were based on the concept of the sublime as put forth by Longinus—that nature was a transcendent element of life, able to excite the imagination and elevate the human spirit to a higher realm of self-awareness and creativity; however, few romantic landscapes were simple pastoral scenes. Many incorporated disturbing elements of the sublime as defined by Burke. This tendency is explained by Kathryn Calley Galitz on the Metropolitan Museum of Art Web site:

In Romantic art, nature—with its uncontrollable power, unpredictability, and potential for cataclysmic extremes —offered an alternative to the ordered world of Enlightenment thought. The violent and terrifying images of nature conjured by Romantic artists recall . . . man's struggle against the awesome power of nature. J.M.W. Turner's 1812 depiction of Hannibal and his army crossing the Alps, in which the general and his troops are dwarfed by the overwhelming scale of the landscape and engulfed in the swirling vortex of snow, embodies the Romantic sensibility in landscape painting.[16]

Landscapes such as *View of Kirchet* by Jean Francois Xavier Roffiaen reflect the romantic concept of nature as a powerful and transcendent force.

From the dramatically beautiful landscapes to gory scenes of horror, romantic symbolism foreshadowed the modern era, in which few limits are placed on artistic expression. Today, even as wars and revolutions continue unabated, modern artists produce work to shock, provoke, and inspire. Whether or not they know it, they are using artistic concepts pioneered by a few dozen artists who lived in a distant time and a different world.

2

The German Roots of Romanticism

Between the late eighteenth and early nineteenth centuries, present-day Germany, then known as the Holy Roman Empire, experienced a romantic renaissance. Musically, it was the age of Mozart, Beethoven, Haydn, and Schubert. In literature, books written by romantic writers Johann Wolfgang von Goethe and Friedrich Schiller and philosopher Immanuel Kant inspired intellectual discussions throughout Europe. Even children's fairy tales published by the Brothers Grimm were a source of romantic inspiration. And in the world of art, painters such as Caspar David Friedrich and Philipp Otto Runge, working in Dresden, created masterpieces that not only exemplified the romantic movement but made that city the center of the romantic school of painting. The works created by the romantics influenced students and teachers, critics and art patrons, and poets, painters, and sculptors who helped spread the philosophy of the romantic movement throughout Europe and the United States.

When the romantic rebellion was established in the Holy Roman Empire, it was not a single, united nation but dozens of small principalities and urban areas called free cities. These regions were controlled by princes, often acting as totalitarian dictators, who tried to outdo one another by building ostentatious castles and forming large, royal courts. It was fashionable within these princely courts to imitate the styles and tastes of the French aristocracy, including the French reverence for classical Greek art and literature, a style venerated by neoclassical artists and critics such as Johann Winckelmann.

Consequently, by the end of the eighteenth century, some German writers, philosophers, and artists were in full rebellion against the Greek influence so beloved by princes and art critics. As journalist Georg Forster wrote in 1790, "Greek figures and Greek gods no longer correspond to the form of the human species; they are as foreign to us as the Greek sounds and names in our poetry."[17]

Storm and Stress

The roots of the German romantic movement may be found among writers who, according to Hugh Honour in *Romanticism*, were "attempting to liberate German arts from French influence."[18] The intense, youthful authors strongly rejected what they perceived as the cold rationalism of the French Enlightenment, beloved by aristocrats and the upper echelon of society. During the 1760s and the 1770s this movement was known as the Sturm und Drang, or Storm and Stress, movement, so named because the work focused on the troubled, traumatic aspects of life.

Followers of this movement believed that happiness was simply unobtainable for those with sensitive artistic temperaments. These authors, according to William Vaughn in *German Romantic Painting*, "followed the path of their emotions to the

Fairy tales collected by German professors Jacob and Wilhelm Grimm contained many romantic elements of horror, deceit, and danger.

ROMANTIC ART AND FAIRY TALES

It is no accident that many romantic paintings contain the fantastical elements of fairy tales. This is due in a large part to Jacob and Wilhelm Grimm, two German professors known as the Brothers Grimm who published fairy tales and folk legends in the early 1800s. The first volume of the Grimms' fairy tales, *Children's and Household Tales*, published in 1808, contained eighty-six stories well known today, including *Little Red Riding Hood*, *The Frog King*, *Cinderella*, *Hansel and Gretel*, and *Rumpelstiltskin*. Many of the stories, which date back to medieval times, fit well into the context of German romanticism. Although many center on innocents, such as children and animals, they contain elements of horror. For example, *Hansel and Gretel* is about two starving children who set forth into the dangerous woods in search of food. They find a witch who tries to fatten them up so she can eat them. The children escape by pushing the witch into a fiery oven. Other tales contain devious wolves, deceitful elves, and wicked siblings. Many take place in wild, moody woodlands or seascapes of the type depicted in romantic paintings.

In the fairy tale Hansel and Gretel, two starving children discover a house made from gingerbread as the occupant, an evil witch, looks on.

point where it brought them into conflict with the existing values of the moribund [declining] society of contemporary Germany."[19]

This feeling of hopelessness was best expressed in the classic work of the Storm and Stress movement, Goethe's *The Sorrows of Young Werther*, published in 1774. The novel, written in the first person and said to be semiautobiographical, is about a sensitive young man, Werther, who meets an enchanting woman named Lotte at a ball. He falls deeply in love with her upon first sight, but she is engaged to Albert, a wealthy man eleven years her senior. Lotte rejects Werther's advances, but over the course of several months Werther builds a close friendship with her and Albert. Finally, the tortured young man, casting reason aside and overtaken by his extreme emotionalism, shoots himself with the Albert's revolver.

Considered a shocking story, *Werther* became an overnight sensation and made Goethe an instant literary celebrity. The book incited a wave of suicides among young German men who believed that the world was an irrational place with no solutions to their despair. This bleak story helped to form the basis of German romanticism. According to David Jay Brown and Rebecca McClen Novick, *Werther* is "[one] of the great influential documents of romanticism." The book "exalts sentiment, even to the point of justifying committing suicide because of unrequited love. The book set a tone and mood much copied by the romantics in their works and often in their personal lives: a fashionable tendency to frenzy, melancholy, world-weariness, and even self-destruction."[20]

"Middle Ages, Christianity, and German-ness"

Romantic painters went beyond the themes of conflict, tragedy, and death found in the literary world. In their rejection of the Enlightenment emphasis on scientific and factual analysis, German romantics believed that religious elation could be found in the adoration of nature and that spirituality could best be expressed in landscapes.

There was also a newfound sense of culturally defined nationalism found in German romanticism. This was expressed by those who believed that the Gothic and Nordic, or northern European, societies were superior to the French or classical Greek cultures. This sentiment was also expressed by Goethe. The year before he published *Werther*, he wrote an essay, *On German Architecture*, that gave new, positive meaning to the word *Gothic*.

Previously, according to Goethe, medieval German architecture was associated with "the ill-defined, the disordered, unnatural, pieced-together, patched-up . . . [and] barbaric."[21] But while studying the architecture of the Gothic Strasbourg Cathedral, Goethe experienced great joy in the work of his countrymen. He also saw the similarities between the majestic spires of the medieval church and the regal pines of the northern European forest. Through his observations of the cathedral, Goethe came to praise the superiority of northern European religion and culture, as Chu explains:

> [He] compared the Christian spirituality of the Gothic cathedral to the pagan physicality of the Classical temple. Unlike Classical buildings, which were carefully planned and measured, Gothic architecture, to Goethe, was instinctive, natural, "felt." The association forged by Goethe between emotion, spirituality, and nature on one hand, and the Middle Ages, Christianity, and German-ness on the other, became one of the central tenets of German Romanticism.[22]

Friedrich's Contemplation of Nature

The romantic melding of Christianity, Gothic architecture, nature, and emotion was exemplified in the work of Caspar David Friedrich. Born in the province of Pomerania in present-day northern Germany and Poland in the same year that *Werther* was published, Friedrich was raised in a strict Protestant household. Like many other young men, he was

GOETHE: THE GREATEST WRITER OF THE GERMAN TRADITION

Although he was not a painter, Johann Wolfgang von Goethe provided the philosophical foundation of the romantic art movement. Jane K. Brown explains his importance:

Johann Wolfgang von Goethe is widely recognized as the greatest writer of the German tradition. The Romantic period in Germany . . . is known as the age of Goethe, and Goethe embodies the concerns of the generation. . . . His stature derives not only from his literary achievements as a lyric poet, novelist, and dramatist but also from his often significant contributions as a scientist (geologist, botanist, anatomist, physicist, historian of science) and as a critic and theorist of literature and of art. He was, finally, such an imposing personality that for the last thirty years of his life he was Germany's greatest cultural monument, serving as an object of pilgrimage from all over Europe and even from the United States and leaving the small town of Weimar a major cultural center for decades after his death. Out of this extraordinary personal presence; out of his overwhelming, almost threatening, literary stature; and out of the rejection of his political position in the turbulence of nineteenth-century German politics, a tradition developed that Goethe's greatness lay in his wisdom rather than in his literary achievement.

Jane K. Brown, "Johann Wolfgang von Goethe," Worldroots.com, http://worldroots.com/brigitte/goethe1.htm.

influenced by Goethe but moreso by a prominent Lutheran pastor Gotthard Ludwig Kosegarten.

This religious leader was also a poet who preached what might be defined as pantheism, a word whose Greek roots mean "all is god." Protestant pantheism, developed by eighteenth-century European philosophers, stated that the universe, nature, and humanity were all part of God. Kosegarten

The paintings of Caspar David Friedrich, such as *Wanderer in a Sea of Fog*, often featured lone figures, with their backs to the viewer, contemplating windswept panoramas.

specifically wrote that people could understand God by spending time alone in the wilderness contemplating nature. Following that belief, Friedrich began painting landscapes early in his career. The artist felt that by faithfully rendering nature on the canvas, he too could become divine: "I must give myself up to all that surrounds me. . . . I must be one with my clouds and rocks, in order to succeed in being what I am. I need nature in order to communicate with nature— and with God."[23]

One of Friedrich's early masterpieces, *Cross in the Mountains*, is an attempt by the artist to commune with both nature and God. Painted in 1808 as an altar piece for a private chapel, the canvas depicts a silhouette of Jesus on the cross at sunset, high on a boulder-strewn mountain. He is surrounded by evergreen trees while beams of light project up into a dramatic sunset. The frame that surrounds the painting resembles a Gothic arch decorated with religious symbols.

In this work, Friedrich expressed his belief that it was possible for an artist to convey spiritual mysticism, drama, and passion in a landscape. He attributed profound meanings to the natural images, claiming that the sunset signifies the fading of the old, pre-Christian world, the mountain represents a mighty, resolute faith, and the evergreen trees symbolize hope.

When *Cross in the Mountains* was briefly displayed in Dresden before Christmas, a heated controversy arose. Critics who subscribed to neoclassical dogma considered it heretical that a landscape painting would contain deep religious meaning or be used in any way for religious purposes. This view was rancorously expressed by Freiherr von Ramdohr, who wrote,

> It would be a veritable presumption if landscape painting were to sneak into the church and creep onto the altar. . . . [We must resist] that mysticism that is now insinuating itself everywhere, and that comes wafting towards us from art . . . philosophy and religion like a narcotic vapor.[24]

Tragedy and Redemption

In other paintings, Friedrich replaced the "narcotic vapor" of religion with extremely morbid and melancholy images such as snow-covered ruins, funeral processions, cemeteries, coffins, and crooked gravestones. Many of the painter's works featured lone figures with their backs to the viewer, dwarfed beneath moody skies on windswept beaches, foggy mountaintops, or towering forests.

There is little doubt that such images were the expression of the introverted painter's personal sadness and depression, conditions attributed to a childhood tragedy. When he was thirteen, Friedrich was ice-skating with his brother, who fell through the ice and drowned as the young man watched helplessly. Critics believe that the icy, watery death is symbolized in one of Friedrich's major works, *The Polar Sea*, painted in 1823–24. The work is described by Norbert Wolf in *Painting of the Romantic Era:*

> The sailing ship crushed by ice floes in a desolate polar landscape can be understood as a symbol of epochal disaster, encompassing both the futility of human effort and the human capacity to hope against all odds. . . . In addition, the image would appear to reflect a tragic experience of the artist's youth, for which he partially blamed himself—the death of his younger brother. . . . Though the sea has frozen to ice and organic nature seems as doomed as the ship, the light-flooded sky and unbounded horizon stand, as so often in Friedrich's work, for faith in redemption.[25]

The redemption in the painting may have been part of Friedrich's attempt to forgive himself for the death of his brother. Certainly his later works—seascapes such as *Evening on the Baltic* and *Chalk Cliffs on Rügen*—depict the natural world with an emotional romanticism that inspires joy and hopefulness. These works were barely appreciated in his day, however, and he lived in dire poverty, depending on the charity of friends and family for survival, until his death in 1840.

This sad end is ironic for an artist who is now recognized as the preeminent painter of the romantic era.

Runge's New Kind of Art

The landscapes of Friedrich are often compared with those of Philipp Otto Runge, and both men share a remarkably similar background. Runge was born in 1777, only three years after Friedrich, and was raised in a conservative Protestant home. Like Friedrich, Runge fell under the influence of Kosegarten and was inspired to create landscapes. Both men attended art school at the Academy of Copenhagen and both moved to Dresden to begin their careers. Unlike Friedrich, however, Runge died when he was only thirty-three, a year younger than Friedrich when he presented *Cross in the Mountains*. In addition, many artistic differences separate the two painters.

The ice floes and shipwreck in *The Polar Sea* by Caspar David Friedrich symbolize desolation and futility. The light-flooded sky promises hope and redemption.

Although Friedrich often added spiritual elements to his landscapes, the paintings were always based on reality, even if it was an idealized realism. Runge, on the other hand, painted imaginative visions of angels, cherubs, and clouds. Runge also painted elaborately illustrated frames around his scenes, creating what is known as picture within a picture. For example, in the 1808 canvas *Morning*, a nude female figure bathed in golden morning light rises from the sea. Above her head, a large lily flower blossoms. The cup of the flower is filled with putti, pudgy babies with wings. The frame around the picture, also painted on the canvas, depicts amaryllis bulbs and flowers and the heavens, what Runge called "the limitless illumination of the universe."[26]

Although *Morning* might be described as a scene from heaven, the painting has no overt religious symbols, such as the Virgin Mary or a crucifix. Instead, *Morning* seems to be a tribute to the spirituality of nature, with dappled sunlight, impossibly blue skies, crashing waves, sprouting bulbs, and blooming flowers holding infants. By presenting this idealized subject matter, Runge was expressing the romantic philosophy that tied veneration for nature to religious euphoria. In 1802, he explained his feelings in mystical terms:

> We stand on the brink of all the religions which have come down from the Catholic. The abstractions are fading away: everything is becoming more airy and light than before, everything gravitates toward landscape. The artists search for something definite in this vagueness and do not know where to start. Some, mistakenly, go back into history, and become confused. But could we not reach the point of highest perfection in a new kind of art, in this art of landscape, and perhaps reach a higher beauty than existed before?[27]

Times of Day

Runge's rhetorical question was soon answered in the century that followed, as landscapes indeed came to be the primary genre in the art world for expressing beauty. Predictions about landscape painting notwithstanding, Runge was a pioneer in another artistic concept called total art, which was meant to create a mystical experience for the viewer. Runge envisioned exhibiting his work in a specially designed Gothic building where music would be played and poetry would be read. Today, artistic installations with art, music, and poetry are common, but in Runge's day such exhibitions were unheard of. In an attempt to make his dream of total art come true, Runge designed other paintings that were meant to be exhibited alongside *Morning*, which originated as a sketch in 1803.

Mystical artist Philipp Otto Runge intended his painting *Morning* to show a connection between religion and the spirituality of nature.

Called "Times of Day," this series included sketches called *Day, Midday, Evening*, and *Night*, all with similar cosmic themes; however, except for *Morning*, "Times of Day" was never finished.

Like Friedrich's, Runge's work was largely misunderstood, which prevented the painter from obtaining commissions. As Runge's brother Joseph wrote, patrons were afraid he might "produce something too mystical, that people would not understand."[28] Despite his ongoing financial struggles, however, Runge, ever the romantic, continued to believe that nature, God, and his own being were at one within him. Eight years before he died of tuberculosis, he wrote to his brother David:

> When the sky above me teems with stars, when the wind blows through the vastness of space, and the wave breaks in the immense night; when above the forest the reddish morning light appears, and the sun begins to illuminate the world; when the valley steams, and I lie tossing in the grass which sparkles with dew; when every leaf and blade of grass teems with life, and the earth comes to life and stirs beneath me, and everything harmonizes in one great chord: then my soul rejoices and soars in the immeasurable space around me. There is no high or low, no time, no beginning or end. I hear and feel the living breath of God Who holds and supports the world, in Whom everything lives and acts—this is our highest feeling: God.[29]

Friedrich's Influence

Although Runge died at an early age and Friedrich fought unsuccessfully to achieve commercial and critical success, both painters were highly influential for a generation of German artists. For example, Carl Gustav Carus met Friedrich in 1818 and became enamored with the painter's romantic style. The following year Carus traveled to Pomerania to study the desolate, frozen scenery that had inspired Friedrich as a youth. Carus, however, was more than an aspiring artist. He was a

ART AND THE HOLY ROMAN EMPIRE

In Nineteenth Century Art, *Petra ten-Doesschate Chu explains the artistic atmosphere of the Holy Roman Empire:*

Unlike most European countries—Britain, France, Spain—where art was centered in the capitals, Germany had no single art center but several. In some of these . . . art patronage was primarily an activity of private citizens who bought paintings for their homes. Artistic training too, was not centralized in Germany as it was in France or Britain, where to attend the academies of Paris or London was the dream of every aspiring artist. Germany had a number of respected academies—in Berlin, Dresden, Düsseldorf, Leipzig, and Munich—each of which had a distinct history and curriculum. . . . If there was a common denominator in German art of the early nineteenth century, it was the importance of religion, in the broadest sense of the word. . . . The spiritual content of German painting, no doubt, was closely related to the burgeoning Romantic movement in German literature. Nearly all German artists of the turn of the eighteenth century seem to have been familiar with the writings of the *Sturm und Drang* (Storm and Stress) group . . . and few remain untouched by their ideas.

Petra ten-Doesschate Chu, *Nineteenth Century Art.* New York: Harry N. Abrams, 2003, pp. 164–65.

distinguished doctor and scientist who later in life became the personal physician to the king of Saxony. After studying with Friedrich, Carus became an exponent of the theory that landscapes could help people grasp the meaning behind life's constant changes. In 1835 he explained that paintings could demonstrate "that there is nothing lawless, insignificant, or accidental in the drift of clouds, the shape of mountains, the anatomy of trees and the motion of waves, but that there lives in all of them a significance and eternal meaning."[30]

With its moody skies, solemn imagery, and supernatural atmosphere, *The Goethe Monument* by Carl Gustav Carus is a classic example of romantic art.

Whatever the philosophical underpinnings of his art, Carus's early works, such as *Moonlight Night Near Rügen*, closely resemble Friedrich's work. Carus, however, painted with more detail than Friedrich, and some of his work has a more realistic edge. Carus's most famous painting, *The Goethe Monument*, is said to pay tribute to both the romantic writer and to Friedrich. Painted in 1832, the canvas shows an imaginary monument with praying angels and a stone harp, dedicated to Goethe. In the center, the writer's sarcophagus is framed by pines and backed by swirling mists. Lonely, rocky peaks both tower over and seem to close in on the monument. As Wolf writes, "Goethe, who devoted himself so intensively to questions of the world and humanity, has been recast in

Carus's picture into an unworldly and lonely Romantic figure. His imaginary grave evokes Romantic yearning . . . an envisioned place of pilgrimage, an altar, a holy of holies."[31]

Karl Friedrich Schinkel is another painter both influenced by Goethe and Friedrich and respected in another field. Schinkel was an esteemed architect whose most famous building, the Old Museum in Berlin, was built between 1823 and 1830 and is still in use today. In his canvas *Gothic Cathedral by the Waterside*, the painter combined elements of his architectural talent with Friedrich's subject matter of Gothic buildings, moody clouds, and sunset lighting.

In addition to art and architecture, Schinkel created theatrical sets. Some of his most fantastic canvas backdrops were used for a new performance of Mozart's *The Magic Flute* in 1816 at the Royal Opera House in Berlin. Surviving paintings of the monumental sets show how Schinkel combined elements of romantic fantasy that were unique in theater at the time. For example, *Starry Sky for the Queen of the Night* depicts an Egyptian queen who appears to be standing on an upturned crescent moon. As in many romantic paintings, the figure is portrayed as small and insignificant compared to the deep blue sky, studded with bands of stars, that arches over the scene.

Human Emotions, God, and the Infinite Cosmos

Before romantic painting gave way to the realism of the second half of the nineteenth century, many German and Austrian painters took part in the romantic revolution pioneered by Friedrich and Runge. Artists such as Ernst Ferdinand Oehme, Georg Friedrich Kersting, and Carl Rottmann all contributed their own visions and interpretations to a style that attempted to meld human emotions with the natural world and Gothic sentiments with God and the infinite cosmos. From this fusion, the romantic pioneers created a wide array of work that helped change the way people looked at—and thought about—themselves and the world around them.

3

Politics and Romance in France

The romantic movement began as a reaction to the notions of the Enlightenment that had dominated European thought since the early eighteenth century. While the romantics embraced an emotional, dramatic, dreamlike, and sometimes morbid view of life, Enlightenment thinkers believed that rational thought, science, and mathematics would solve society's problems. The clash between these two competing schools of thought was nowhere more obvious than in France, home to the widely esteemed Enlightenment philosophers Voltaire and Denis Diderot. These men used wit, allegory, and clever fiction to expose the injustices and oppression perpetrated by the monarchy. Ironically, such enlightened beliefs in universal reason, order, and justice formed the philosophical basis for the bloody, chaotic French Revolution in 1789. Although the revolution was initially fomented by those seeking democracy, in 1793 French revolutionaries instituted the Reign of Terror. During these eleven months, King Louis XVI, his wife, Marie Antoinette, and seventeen thousand civilians were sent to the guillotine.

The Heroic Style of Jacques-Louis David

During this violent period in France, the painter Jacques-Louis David, born in 1748, dominated the art world. David first rose to fame as a strong supporter of the French Revolution, and he was granted great influence because of his friendship with Maximilien de Robespierre, who led the Reign of Terror. As the self-appointed minister of art, David abolished the prestigious French Royal Academy of Painting and established an alternative school, the Arts Commune, over which he presided. In this role, David used his talents to support the government by designing military uniforms and organizing political events with opulent theatrical staging.

The drama and excitement of the French Revolution inspired David to develop what is called the heroic style, which

The heroic style of *The Intervention of the Sabine Women* by Jacques-Louis David combines elements of French neoclassicism with German romanticism.

combined neoclassicism with elements of the romantic art seen in Germany. David's paintings of this period depict historic moments in the revolution and portray French revolutionaries as brave, noble, nearly godlike characters.

When Robespierre himself was sent to the guillotine in 1794, David was jailed for a short time. During this period, the artist made sketches for a monumental work, *The Intervention of the Sabine Women*, that depicted a battle scene from the legendary founding of Rome. Five years later, David finally finished the *Sabine Women*. At a highly publicized showing at the famous Paris art museum the Louvre, the huge canvas—13 by 18 feet (4 by 5.5m) —was hung on the long wall of a

As Napoleon's official painter, Jacques-Louis David portrayed the French emperor as fearless and heroic in paintings such as *Bonaparte Crossing the St. Bernard Pass.*

gallery and a large mirror was placed on the opposite wall. In one of the first exhibitions of the type Runge would later label total art, viewers were able to look into the mirror and see themselves reflected as part of the heroic scene.

The same year that David displayed his monumental work, a young general named Napoleon Bonaparte took over the government and in the following year named himself First Consul, or emperor, of France. David quickly renounced his revolutionary past and aligned himself with the charismatic new emperor. Recognizing the propaganda value of heroic art, Napoleon named David his official painter. The artist responded by creating a series of works that portrayed Napoleon as fearless, gallant, and saintly. Clark describes David's 1800 painting of Napoleon crossing the Alps into Italy, *Bonaparte Crossing the St. Bernard Pass:* "[No] man has ever been made to look more heroic than the First Consul, in a totally unrealistic but stunningly effective memorial to his greatest exploit, crossing the Great St. Bernard."[32] In the following years, David continued to paint the emperor in the heroic style in such paintings as the grandiose *Consecration of the Emperor Napoleon I and Coronation of the Empress Josephine* in 1808 and *Napoleon in His Study* in 1812. When Napoleon's reign ended in 1814, however, David was banished from France. He lived in Belgium during the last ten years of his life.

Napoleon's Painter

Jacques-Louis David's heroic style was not intrinsically romantic, but his influence was widely felt. As Vaughn writes in *Romanticism and Art*, David "was demonstrably better than any of his rivals; better produced, more capable of appeal and inspiration. Old opponents . . . changed their style to fall in with his; while for younger generations . . . he remained the father of French painting."[33] Thus, David's paintings form the roots of the French style of romanticism, which developed between 1800 and 1860. In addition, David was also a notable art teacher, and several of his students are closely identified with the romantic style.

One of David's pupils, Antoine-Jean Gros, was taught by the master in 1785 at the age of fourteen. In later years, Gros was forced to leave his homeland because of his teacher's association with the French Revolution. In 1796, while studying in Italy, Gros met Napoleon and soon began painting canvases for the general. In the following years, Gros followed the traditions of his teacher and portrayed the emperor as a dashing, heroic figure. As he had done earlier with David, Napoleon was quick to exploit the political value of Gros's work. Clark analyzes Gros's monumental work *Bonaparte Visiting the Plague-Stricken at Jaffa*, created in 1804:

> Gros made his first great contribution to the Napoleonic legend—a vast canvas of Bonaparte visiting men stricken with bubonic plague in the hospital at Jaffa [in present-day Israel]. As propaganda the subject

is a stroke of genius, and I incline to think that it was invented by Bonaparte himself. It is not at first sight an assertion of power but of compassion; and yet at a deeper level it recalls the power of the anointed king to cure illness at a touch—and [gives] the image a heroic dimension . . . for General Bonaparte to touch these infected bodies was an act of sublime courage. This is the first example of romantic realism.[34]

Gros continued to create paintings of Napoleon while refining the romantic realist style. His next work, *Napoleon on the Battlefield at Eylan*, painted in 1808, contains several elements of romanticism. The moody sky is filled with smoke from the battle, while dead bodies lie in a pile in the foreground. The Poles and Lithuanians purportedly liberated by Napoleon surround him, dramatically kneeling in thanks. The painting also contains elements that may be interpreted as political romanticism in that it implies the artist's opinion of the event. Although at face value it appears to be an homage to the heroism of Bonaparte, it also graphically depicts the horrors of war. Ironically, the painting also has imagery strikingly similar to that in Goya's *The Third of May*, a painting that depicts Napoleon's soldiers as butchers and war criminals.

Whatever their propaganda value, Gros' paintings caused a sensation, and the painter surpassed David as France's most honored artist. Moreover, his dramatic compositions and bright colors had a great influence on the romantic painters of the day. After the fall of the emperor, however, Gros never matched his earlier glory as Napoleon's romantic painter. The artist's popularity was quickly overtaken by those he had influenced, such as Eugène Delacroix and Théodore Géricault. In 1835, despondent over his failures, Gros drowned himself in 3 feet (1m) of water in the Seine River.

"Old, but Not Ancient"

After Napoleon was driven from power in 1814, Louis XVIII of the royal Bourbon dynasty became king of France. This period, called the Restoration, was a fertile time for romantic

painters. The king reestablished the Royal Academy and gave it a new name, the Académie des Beaux-Arts (Academy of Fine Arts). Members of its board, which included fourteen painters, six sculptors, eight architects, and eight musicians, among others, dominated the arts in France and controlled admissions to the School of Fine Arts. Board members selected the school's faculty and organized student art contests. The academy also appointed judges to the prestigious art exhibition called the Salon. Any French artist hoping for fame and financial success was therefore obligated to attend the School of Fine Arts and win exhibition space at the Salon.

Although the Salon was initially controlled by neoclassicists, the romantic style of art gained popularity, first appearing at the annual exhibitions in 1819. This might have been a result of a growing public acceptance of romanticism, a change that was due in large part to a best-selling book, *Germany*, published in 1810 by French author Germaine de Staël. In

Napoleon on the Battlefield at Eylan by Jean-Antoine Gros depicts the horrors of war with romantic elements such as smoky skies, shattered bodies, and dramatically posed figures.

Germany de Staël argued that classical Greek culture, mimicked by neoclassical artists, was foreign to French culture, which had a storied medieval past. She wrote: "Romantic literature is the only one that is still susceptible to being perfected because, as it has its roots in our own soil, it is the only one that can grow and revive itself. It expresses our religion, it recalls our history, its origin is old, but not ancient."[35] This was the same argument that leading romantics had made regarding Germany, where the romantic movement was in full flower at the time de Staël's book was published.

Romanticism was given further definition by another French writer, Henri Beyle, who used the Germanic pen name Stendhal. In a detailed review of the Salon of 1824, Stendhal declared that the heroic school of Jacques-Louis David was dead because the style could portray only the human body, not the soul. Stendhal also stated that French artists should not follow the same path as the German romantics, who revered the medieval past. Instead of portraying ancient history, Stendhal argued, French artists should use romantic painting techniques to render the present: "Romanticism in all the arts is what represents the men of today and not the men of those remote, heroic times, which probably never existed anyway."[36]

In addition to charting a divergent course for the French romantics, Stendhal proposed another concept: Artists should not make paintings to satisfy the tastes of royalty and aristocrats but should instead create art that would be appreciated by the majority of average citizens. This was a revolutionary idea at the time, but those who followed it quickly loosened the tight grasp that the Academy of Fine Arts had on French art.

Vernet's "Immediacy and Truth"

According to Stendhal, Horace Vernet was the painter most capable of producing romantic art focused on this new subject matter. Vernet's very birth had a romantic element. He was born in the Louvre in 1789 when his father, who was a painter, and his mother were hiding there during the French Revolution. Early in his career, Vernet painted large, heroic

MADAME DE STAËL INTRODUCES ROMANTICISM TO FRANCE

Germaine de Staël was an author whose book Germany *popularized the romantic movement in France. The following biography of de Staël, by Petri Liukkonen, is excerpted from the Pegasos Web site:*

French-Swiss writer, woman of letters, early champion of women's rights, who was considered among Napoléon's major opponents, [Germaine de Staël] spent much of her life in exile. . . . Germaine Necker was born in [1766 in] Paris to Swiss Protestant parents. . . . The young [woman] studied privately at home, and grew up attending the salon of her mother, Suzanne (Curchod) Necker. In her childhood Germaine met such famous figures as [historian and scholar] Edward Gibbon . . . [and Enlightenment philosophers] Denis Diderot and Jean d'Alembert. . . .

In 1807 she traveled in Germany where she interviewed Goethe, Schiller . . . and other leading intellectuals of the country. . . . *[Germany,]* a study of German culture, appeared in 1810. [The] minister of police banned the book as an anti-French work . . . [because it] described the German people as musical and more interested in [greater] ideas than [war]. . . . Mme de Staël advocated the idea, which became a cliché, that the [neoclassical] was descended from the Pagan Roman past, dominant in southern Europe, and the romantic from the knightly and Christian world of the North.

Petri Liukkonen, "Madame de Staël," Pegasos, 2002. www.kirjasto.sci.fi/stael.htm.

battle scenes of the Napoleonic wars. By the 1820s, his monumental scenes incorporated many romantic elements, with smoky skies dominating the view above small, seemingly insignificant battalions of soldiers engaged in senseless, bloody battle. In 1822, Vernet submitted two canvases to the Salon: *The Battle of Jemappes*, showing a revolutionary victory, and *The*

Defense of Barrière de Clichy, depicting Napoleon's last stand. Both were rejected because Salon judges feared they might revive memories of the revolutionary ideals and Napoleon's heroism, which would have threatened the stability of the Restoration monarchy.

Stung by this denunciation, Vernet decided to display the paintings in his studio, and the exhibit drew huge crowds eager to see the controversial work essentially censored by the Salon. As a result, Vernet became famous nearly overnight. By the time of the next Salon in 1824, the academy had little choice but to allow the painter to exhibit more than three dozen of the paintings he submitted.

One of Vernet's paintings shown at the 1824 Salon is said to exemplify the French romantic style. *The Battle of Montmirail*, which depicts the clash between French and

Horace Vernet's *Battle of Jemappes* was initially considered too controversial to be displayed in the official Salon.

Russian troops on February 11, 1814, fits several romantic criteria, according to Stendahl. The subject was a relatively recent occurrence, the work was painted in dramatically contrasting colors to evoke strong feelings, and it showed a gritty scene of intractable hell on earth, where dozens of combatants are fighting, bleeding, and dying on the ground. Lacking a single redeeming figure or action, the painting signaled an end to the heroic style. As Chu writes,

> No longer was art expected to educate and edify the viewer by means of moralizing subjects and noble, idealized forms. Instead, it was to affect the spectator at a visceral level through subjects that evoked strong emotions . . . and forms that appealed powerfully to the senses. . . . Vernet's journalistic approach lends to his work a sense of immediacy and truth that is distinct from Gros's carefully constructed propaganda image.[37]

The "Obstacles and Difficulties" of Théodore Géricault

Although Vernet was a pioneer of romanticism in France, he is not as well known as his associate, Théodore Géricault. Like Vernet, Géricault painted relatively recent events, scenes of war, and tragedies that sometimes antagonized Restoration rulers because of their political viewpoint. Géricault, however, took a less journalistic approach to painting and focused more on hopelessness, gloom, and despair.

Géricault himself seems to have had little cause to celebrate misery. He was born into a wealthy family in 1791, had the talent to study with the revered Vernet in Paris, and was able to afford to live in Italy and study the old masters from 1816 to 1818. Géricault was also tall, muscular, handsome, and so attractive to women that he shaved his head, he claimed, to discourage their attentions. With so many assets in his life, Géricault complained that he lacked the experience of suffering; however,

The Raft of the Medusa by Théodore Géricault is based on a real shipwreck that left victims abandoned at sea without food or water.

he was determined to explore it in his works, stating, "Obstacles and difficulties which repel mediocre men are a necessity and nourishment to genius. They mature and elevate [brilliance], when in an easier road it would have remained cold."[38]

Géricault's first major exploration of human suffering, *The Raft of the* Medusa, was both a record of a horrifying event and an attack on the government. The event that inspired the painting took place on July 2, 1816, when the ship *Medusa* ran aground a few miles from shore while transporting soldiers and settlers to the French colony of Senegal in Africa. Because of bureaucratic incompetence, the ship did not have enough lifeboats for all the passengers. The captain, an aristocrat, ordered the ship's carpenter to strip off pieces of the ship and construct a huge raft.

One woman and 149 men were ordered onto the raft, which was ostensibly to be towed ashore by sailors rowing lifeboats; however, the sailors, eager to reach the shore, cut the tow ropes. Although the raft was not far from shore, it drifted out to sea with no food, water, or protection from the elements for its unfortunate passengers. During the following days, a catalog of horrors ensued on the raft: madness, death, murder, and cannibalism. When the group was finally rescued after fifteen days at sea, only 15 of the original 150 people were alive. Five died after they were rescued.

The Bourbon government tried to cover up the incident and for a year it was kept secret. The captain was quietly put on trial but received a lenient sentence; however, two survivors, a doctor and an engineer, wrote a book about the incident that quickly became a sensational best seller throughout Europe. In France, the book generated widespread anger and criticism concerning government negligence and corruption.

After copies of the book were seized by authorities, Géricault decided to paint a picture of the tragedy to express his revulsion. Before making the first sketches, however, he interviewed survivors and even sought out the *Medusa*'s carpenter, persuading him to make a scale model of the raft. Moving to a room near a hospital, Géricault spent months studying the expressions and body postures of men who were in the throes of death.

Heroic Desolation

Mixing realism and romanticism, Géricault made a series of sketches. One depicted a mutiny on the raft as the jumble of men fought among themselves; another showed survivors eating the dead. A small painting pictured the detached heads of a man and a woman, while another canvas was titled *Severed Legs and an Arm*. Finally, after eighteen months of obsessive work on the project, the artist chose to paint a scene portraying a moment when the survivors could see a possible rescue ship on the horizon—a ship that did not see the raft and thus did not save the victims.

Embracing the appalling drama of the false hope of rescue, Géricault painted a large canvas, 16 by 23 feet (5 by 7m). In this depiction of dire, unthinkable human suffering, the raft fills the entire painting. Bodies of the dead, diseased, and dying

THE MORBID WORK OF THÉODORE GÉRICAULT

When Théodore Géricault was working on The Raft of the *Medusa, he wanted to portray the details of agony and suffering correctly. In* Romanticism, *Jean Clay describes the artist's ghoulish quest for accuracy:*

In the course of his preparatory research for *The Raft of the* Medusa, Géricault undertook to capture the most daunting aspects of illness and death. . . . [In] some ten "amphitheater subjects" devoted to human remains, Géricault presents us with… a deliberate confrontation with the intolerable, an attempt to express through painting a fascinating horror of death. "It was in [Beaujon Hospital]," wrote his biographer Clément, "that he studied with avid curiosity every phase of suffering, from the first attacks to the final agony, and all the marks that it left on the human body. There he found models who did not have to feign physical distress or moral anxiety, the ravages of sickness or the terrors of death. He arranged to have the interns and attendants supply him with cadavers and amputated members." Thus Géricault was able to take home and keep the head of a guillotined thief as well as a pair of legs and an arm.

In order to realistically portray human suffering in The Raft of the *Medusa, Théodore Géricault studied the expressions and body postures of the dead and dying.*

Jean Clay, *Romanticism*. New York: Vendome Press, 1981, p. 292.

in the foreground seem to spill off the canvas. Several of the figures express hope, however, reaching their arms or waving shirts in the general direction of the unseen, and unseeing, ship.

When *The Raft of the* Medusa was displayed at the 1819 Salon, reactions were mixed. Because of its political content, critics were afraid to praise it. In addition, the painting was unusual because artists of that time most often reserved monumental works for heroic soldiers, aristocrats, kings, and queens. Géricault's depiction of average people suffering for petty reasons was unknown in the French art world, as Honour explains:

> As published accounts of the wreck made abundantly plain, the men on the raft were not heroes in any normal sense of the word. Neither Spartan courage nor Stoic self-control was displayed by any of them: they had behaved as men all too frequently do in moments of crisis, and those who survived did so simply from a crude and animal urge to live. They suffered atrociously, but in no good or noble cause: they were victims of . . . incompetence, not of human or divine malevolence. But, by painting them as he did, Géricault raised the plight of the ship-wrecked to a level of universal significance, compelling the public to question their attitudes to the perennial problems of heroism, hope, despair and suffering, and providing only a disturbingly ambiguous answer.[39]

Géricault continued to focus on hopelessness and depression. In 1822, he began painting a series of portraits of mentally ill people with titles such as *Man Suffering from Delusions of Military Rank, Portrait of a Woman Suffering from Obsessive Envy, Portrait of a Child Kidnapper*, and *Portrait of a Kleptomaniac.* Géricault too was afflicted, not only with depression, but with physical ailments such as tubercular infections and the lingering pains from a serious riding accident. As his death approached, Géricault felt he had failed as an artist. According to Vaughn, however, the painter had a major impact on the world of romantic art:

Géricault felt that . . . *Medusa* seemed too incomplete a record of his aspirations. Yet in its strange morbidity, its heroic desolation . . . he had created a path for the Romantics to follow, and had resolutely shown that the bizarre and the topical were not simply a matter for minor genres, but were of central importance to an age of disenchantment.[40]

The Exquisite Color of Delacroix

Géricault died in 1824 at the age of thirty-three. Soon after, another artist, Eugène Delacroix, "was enlisted willy nilly into the Romantic coterie,"[41] as he put it. The cause of his enlistment was the acceptance by the Salon of his painting *The Massacre at Chios*, a depiction of an incident in 1822 in which twenty thousand Greeks, seeking to gain independence, were killed by Turks on the island of Chios. The timing of Delacroix's recognition has led many critics over the years to associate his work with that of Géricault, and there are similarities between the two painters. Both, for example, painted scenes that had political viewpoints; however, Delacroix, born in 1798, is said to be a better painter and was certainly much more prolific. Over the course of his career he produced more than 850 paintings and great numbers of drawings. Most of these lack the overt emotional drama produced by Géricault and the subject matter tends toward historical and literary scenes, rather than recent events.

Whatever the degree of Géricault's influence, *The Massacre at Chios* firmly placed Delacroix in the company of the greatest romantic painters. Today, critics praise his striking use of color and contrast and his use of light and shadow. As Wolf writes, "Delacroix casts a veil of glowing, exquisite color, and renders the desolate yet light-flooded landscape in a free and fluent manner that was completely new in France at the time."[42]

Critics, however, roundly condemned *The Massacre at Chios* for its pessimistic depiction of doomed men, women,

The Massacre at Chios by Eugène Delacroix was praised for its use of color and shadow, and criticized for its grim subject matter.

Delacroix Describes The Death of Sardanapalus

The Death of Sardanapalus, by Eugène Delacroix, depicts a hedonistic Assyrian king having his wives and horses killed as rebels overtake his palace. The scene in the painting, said to be the artist's most controversial work, was described by Delacroix in the Salon catalog of 1828:

The rebels besiege [the king] in his palace. . . . Reclined on a superb bed above an immense funeral pyre, Sardanapalus orders his eunuchs and palace officers to slaughter his wives, his pages, even his favorite horses and dogs; none of these objects which have served his pleasure was to survive him. . . . Aischeh, a Bactrian woman, did not wish to suffer a slave to kill her, and hung herself from the columns supporting the vault. . . . Baleah [on the right], cupbearer of Sardanapalus, at last set fire to the funeral pyre and threw himself upon it.

Quoted in Petra ten-Doesschate Chu, *Nineteenth Century Art.* New York: Harry N. Abrams, 2003, p. 213.

and children, waiting to die at the hands of Turkish soldiers. Stendahl said that the painting "erred on the side of excess,"[43] while Gros derisively said that the canvas should be titled *The Massacre of Painting.* Despite the criticism, Delacroix sold the painting to the French government for the then-huge sum of six thousand francs.

Delacroix's next major work in 1828 did little to alleviate the criticism. A painting the artist referred to as his second massacre, *The Death of Sardanapalus* was also called garish and extravagant. The work, which depicts a scene inspired by the poem *Sardanapalus* by Lord Byron, shows an ancient Assyrian king committing suicide after killing his wives and horses and having his room set afire. Describing the emotionalism of the work, Chu writes, "If paintings could make a sound, this one would be filled with screams, shouts, horses neighing, and the clanging of metal pots; if they gave off a scent, it would reek of sweat, blood, and fire."[44]

Delacroix's later work focused more on the exotic than the controversial. After spending six months in North Africa in 1832, he spent much of the rest of his life creating romantic masterpieces depicting the lives and customs of the Arab people, including *The Fanatics of Tangier, The Sultan of Morocco and His Entourage, The Lion Hunt in Morocco*, and *Arab Saddling His Horse*. By the time of his death in 1863, Delacroix was hailed as the greatest French romantic painter. His use of color was later said to have influenced impressionist painters such as Claude Monet and modern artists such as Pablo Picasso. With roots in both classicism and the heroic style of the Napoleonic painters, Delacroix's romantic work provided an artistic bridge between the eighteenth and twentieth centuries.

4

A Different Type of Revolution in Great Britain

The views of the romantics were widely accepted by the general public in Great Britain between 1760 and 1860. Whereas revolutions and rebellions roiled social foundations in France, the clash between romantics and Enlightenment philosophers was not as aggressive or as harsh in England. As Graham Hough writes in *The Last Romantics*, "Nineteenth-century England is notorious for having reform bills instead of revolutions, and there is little of the ferocious Continental antagonism between clericals and non-clericals, liberals and reactionaries."[45]

The British also had less antagonism toward their rulers. Although the nation was ruled by monarchs, they did not have absolute authority. Unlike French monarchs, British kings and queens shared power with the prime minister and the two houses of Parliament: the House of Commons, whose members are directly elected by British citizens, and the House of Lords, whose members are unelected aristocrats. During the romantic era, Parliament was the most democratic governing institution in Europe.

Perhaps because of Great Britain's calmer social environment, romanticism there was seen in a more positive light than on the European continent. Rather than being viewed as a reaction against Enlightenment philosophies, romanticism was associated with the Enlightenment and with people who possessed a spirit of adventure, a sense of wonder, and an active imagination. As Cummings explains,

> To dig up the monuments of antiquity, and with the discovered fragments to recreate a vision of Greece, Rome, or medieval Europe, is romantic. . . . To be infatuated with and to possess an unslakeable appetite for the new, the unusual and the unknown, is romantic. To covet the exotic, to take delight in grottoes, volcanoes, glaciers, folk-tales, Icelandic sagas, Greek myths, unexplored historical periods and literatures is romantic. To examine emotional responses, to catalogue them, to describe, analyze, recreate, and enter into psychological experiences of every variety is romantic. To explore the entire range of human experience as it has been handed down in poetry, fables, folk-tales, and other literary form . . . is romantic. To take delight in the world and

John Constable's *Old Sarum* depicts a mound built at the site of an ancient city near the painter's home in Suffolk, England.

in all facets of experience with every sense alert and every faculty vibrating is the essence of the romantic point of view.[46]

The values of the romantics were palatable to the rich and powerful in Great Britain because the period between 1760 and 1860 was a time of great prosperity for the nation. England was the world's greatest power at the time, and money flowed into the nation from Britain's colonial domination of North America, India, northern Africa, and elsewhere. Although Great Britain lost its American colonies during the time that the romantic movement was becoming firmly established, the Industrial Revolution was creating a large number of middle-class families while enriching the aristocracy.

Because of the thriving economy, art patronage was widespread in Great Britain. In the early nineteenth century, collecting canvases by English artists was fashionable among the wealthy. The middle class also lent support to artists by attending private exhibitions where admission fees were charged. As the artists enriched themselves, they were able to support professional societies and art academies such as the Society of Artists of Great Britain, the Free Society of Artists, and the Royal Academy. The numerous London art societies were in friendly competition with each other. Each vied to present the most innovative artists—those who would draw the largest crowds.

The Five Techniques

Since British artists possessed a degree of respect and power, they were able to follow their creative impulses without great fear of retribution from officials, critics, or society at large. This freedom allowed them to explore a wide range of subject matter and gave their work great diversity. Cummings describes five prevailing underpinnings of the earliest stages of British romantic art:

First is an unprecedented interest in the scientific investigation of nature and its application to works of art. The second is the thorough investigation of the

past, not only through the use of literary descriptions but also by using the technique of archaeological verification. Third is the more critical reading of literary texts in search of heightened emotional experience with the accompanying discovery . . . of a wide variety of new literary sources. Fourth is an unprecedented and almost bewildering fascination with the present, leading artists not only to greater involvement in portraiture, topography, and current events, but even to criticism and caricature of their own society. Fifth is an intensified concentration on psychological responses, the emotions and the emotional. . . . This interest included an emphasis on the imagination and extended to the scientific study of the nervous system.[47]

George Stubbs often depicted brutal aspects of nature, such as the two horses fighting in the painting *The Combat*.

One of the earliest British romantic artists, George Stubbs, born in 1724, was a master of the first element mentioned by Cummings. His interest in combining the scientific with the artistic led him to study human anatomy at the York County Hospital and later spend eighteen months dissecting horses in

Horace Walpole, who wrote the first Gothic novel, *The Castle of Otranto*, was captivated by Gothic architecture, and he had nearly unlimited resources to pursue his interest. In 1747, Walpole bought a country house called Strawberry Hill in Twickenham, near London, and turned it into a medieval Gothic fantasy. He enlarged the house into an enormous castle and added towers, battlements, and hundreds of differently shaped medieval-style windows with painted and stained glass. Inside the massive castle, individual rooms were designed in varying historical styles to allow Walpole and his friends to imagine life in the past. In 1774, Walpole published a detailed description of the house in order to promote Gothic architecture among England's high society.

Walpole's books doubtlessly inspired William Beckford, a wealthy novelist, travel writer, art critic, and politician. Between 1796 and 1807, Beckford indulged his fascination with the Gothic by creating Fonthill Abbey in the southern English county of Wiltshire. Using nearly one thousand laborers working day and night, he built a large Gothic monastery. In the center of the structure, workers constructed a tower nearly 300 feet (92m) high, which dramatically collapsed in 1825.

William Beckford indulged his Gothic fantasies by constructing Fonthill Abbey in southern England.

a rented barn. The result of this study was the 1766 book *The Anatomy of the Horse*, filled with Stubbs's detailed drawings.

When *The Anatomy of the Horse* was discovered by aristocratic sportsmen, Stubbs was able to launch a lucrative artistic career as a painter of thoroughbred horses for huntsmen. Like many romantics, however, Stubbs believed that his main inspiration should come from the natural world. Sometimes cruel aspects of nature inspired Stubbs's work. For example, his 1765 painting *A Lion Attacking a Horse* depicts a terrified white horse attempting to fight off a ferocious lion that has jumped on its back and is tearing into its flesh. The painting features many elements typically seen in later romantic paintings: a moody sky; a scene of revulsion and horror; an exotic element, represented by the lion; and an emotional struggle between good and evil, symbolized by a beautiful animal and a predatory beast.

The Grotesque and Ghastly

A Lion Attacking a Horse was finished the same year that Horace Walpole published *The Castle of Otranto*. The book was the first of what the English called "Gothick" novels. The author's preface to the novel describes it as containing "miracles, visions, necromancy [communication with the dead], dreams, and other preternatural events."[48] Walpole, who was fascinated with Gothic architecture, used his novel to combine mystery and horror. The book became a best seller and aroused among the English public a vision of the Gothic era that emphasized the grisly, grotesque, and fantastic.

The Castle of Otranto proved an inspiration for later Gothic horror stories such as Mary Shelley's *Frankenstein*, Ann Radcliffe's *The Romance of the Forest*, and countless tales by American author Edgar Allan Poe. According to an Internet review of the book by horror critic Keith Parkins, "*The Castle of Otranto* is a little over the top. . . . It contains all the set pieces of Gothic fiction, the crumbling Gothic castle, [and the] frightened [young woman] fleeing through a long subterranean passage [that] has almost become the trademark of the horror movie."[49]

The Castle of Otranto was also inspirational for many romantic artists, who often combined beauty and horror as a way of depicting the sublime, the philosophy of painting repellent images to intensify the emotional experience. Joseph Wright, a painter from Derby in the Midlands north of London, typifies the sublime style in his painting *The Old Man and Death*, based on a story taken from Aesop's fables, written in Greece in the sixth century B.C.

The story tells of an old man who is so weary from carrying a bundle of sticks that he calls on death to relieve him of his burden. In Wright's 1773 painting, a frightened old man is depicted fending off a skeleton whose arms are outstretched in an offer of help. The background is filled with romantic elements, including billowing clouds, a beautiful pastoral woodland, the banks of a lake or stream, and the ruins of an ancient castle. Cummings describes how this work of art makes use of some of the five defining sources of romantic art:

> Part of the rationale of this picture . . . and of the beginnings of romantic art, is that the painter has thought carefully and freshly about the text and has interpreted it literally and more faithfully than illustrators who have preceded him. Wright . . . [presents] the incident with palpable clarity and attention to naturalistic detail. It is in his careful rethinking of the text and its literal interpretation that Wright achieves the necessary degree of emotional intensity. Fantasy is introduced in the setting by means of Gothic ruins overgrown with vines and the moss-laden trunks of half-dead trees.[50]

Fuseli's Nightmares

Some art historians believe that *The Old Man and Death* provided inspiration to Henry Fuseli, a Swiss-born painter who lived and worked in London. Fuseli created *The Nightmare* in 1780, and critics agree that the canvas is one of the most stunning examples of the romantic vision of the sublime. *The*

The melding of images of horror and beauty in *The Nightmare* made Henry Fuseli an overnight sensation when the painting was exhibited in London in 1781.

Nightmare shows a virginal young woman asleep on a bed. Her arms and head hang uncomfortably over the side, a pose that conveys that she is having a bad dream. A nasty looking monster known as a bog fiend or *mara*—believed at the time to cause nightmares—perches on the woman's stomach. Behind the woman, the *mara*'s female steed, according to Cummings a literal "night-mare,"[51] stares at the woman with eyes glowing like burning coals. This work has a contradictory effect upon the viewer: The pose of the striking young woman generates

A GALLERY OF HORRORS

Henry Fuseli was one of the most prominent romantic painters in England. Depicting scenes of Gothic horror and classical fantasy, Fuseli's canvases shocked and frightened viewers. Fuseli, however, was a mild-mannered, slightly built man. In the following description of Fuseli and his work, painter Benjamin Robert Haydon articulates distress, horror, and revulsion, perhaps unintentionally expressing the emotions most venerated by romantic artists:

I followed the maid into a gallery or showroom, enough to frighten anyone at twilight. Galvanized devils—malicious witches brewing their incantations—Satan bridging Chaos, and springing upwards like a pyramid of fire—Lady Macbeth—Paolo and Francesca—Falstaff and Mrs. Quickly—humour, pathos, terror, blood and murder, met one at every look! I expected the floor to give way—I fancied Fuseli himself to be a giant. I heard his footsteps and saw a little bony hand slide round the edge of the door, followed by a little white-headed, lion-faced man in an old flannel dressing-gown tied round his waist with a piece of rope and upon his head the bottom of Mrs. Fuseli's work-basket.... Weak minds he destroyed. They mistook his wit for reason, his indelicacy for breeding, his swearing for manliness, and his infidelity for strength of mind.

Quoted in John Piper, *British Romantic Artists.* London: Collins, 1946, p. 28.

emotions such as concern or even lust, while the threatening bog fiend repels and creates a sense of fear or shame.

When *The Nightmare* was shown in the Royal Academy Exhibition in 1781, viewers were shocked by the images of horror and eroticism. The controversial nature of the painting made Fuseli an overnight sensation. In the years that followed, Fuseli created vivid, intense paintings depicting witches, fairies, giants, Satan, figures of death, and creatures that combined animal and human features. The painter's subject matter was so disturbing that it prompted Walpole to label him "horribly mad."[52] Fuseli also drew his inspiration from literary sources. One of his works, *Titania and Bottom*, was based on *A Midsummer-Night's Dream* by William Shakespeare. A series of forty paintings, including *Satan and Death* and *Separated by Sin*, was based on *Paradise Lost* by the seventeenth-century poet John Milton.

Throughout his life, Fuseli created more than two hundred major canvases, but exhibited only a small percentage of his work. His style transcended romanticism and anticipated the twentieth-century style of surrealism, which emphasized the unconscious mind. As Chu explains, surrealistic works are similar to Fuseli's paintings because they "seem to relate to dreams; but instead of representing the dream 'from the outside,' they seem to draw inspiration from within"[53] the inner reaches of the mind.

William Blake the Mythmaker

When Fuseli was painting *Nightmare*, he befriended William Blake, who lived near him. Fuseli's work undoubtedly influenced his neighbor, but Blake was also a prolific poet and visionary artist in his own right.

Born in London in 1757, Blake was first introduced to art at the age of fourteen, when he worked as a printmaker and engraver. Blake later used his engraving skills to publish hand-made books of his poems, which were printed alongside or entwined among the illustrations. The first two books Blake produced, *Songs of Innocence* in 1789 and *Songs of Experience* in

1794, were companion pieces. Each page contained art and text etched into a copper plate, using a unique method Blake invented himself. After the page was printed in a single color, Blake and his wife, Catherine, undertook the time-consuming process of coloring the illustrations with watercolor paints, a technique that the artist called illuminated printing. In these books, according to *An Introduction to William Blake* by Alfred Kazin,

> Blake was artist and poet; he designed his poems to form a single picture. . . . He designed his poems in such a way that the words on the line seemed to grow like flowerheads out of a thicket. Each hand-printed letter of script, each vine trailing a border between the lines, each moving figure above, beside, and below the page mounts and unites to form some visible representation of the inner life of man—seen in phases of the outward nature.[54]

The poems in *Songs of Innocence* and *Songs of Experience* resemble nursery rhymes—and the drawings seem aimed at children; however, the visual simplicity belies the meaning behind the work. For example, in characteristic romantic fashion, these companion volumes emphasize contrasting desires and emotions. In the poem "Divine Image" from *Songs of Innocence*, Blake writes that humanity embodies "Mercy, Pity, Peace, and Love." In a poem of the same name from *Songs of Experience*, Blake writes:

> *Cruelty has a human heart,*
> *And Jealousy a human face;*
> *Terror the human form divine,*
> *And Secrecy the human dress.*[55]

Blake's contrasting visions of mercy and cruelty, peace and terror, may have been influenced by his political views. As a strong supporter of the French Revolution at first, Blake was hopeful and idealistic about the struggle. His feelings turned to dismay, however, during the horrific Reign of Terror.

Aside from his political interests, Blake considered himself a visionary and a prophet based on hallucinatory experiences that were sometimes pleasant and at other times alarming. As a child, Blake was prone to visions in which angels appeared in treetops or among farmworkers in a field. Later in life, Blake had a terrifying experience that sent him screaming from the room when he believed that he saw God's head appear in his window. These occurrences had a profound effect on Blake's later poetry, which he wrote in the style of an ancient prophet and apocalyptic visionary.

Having learned about the self-destructive tendencies of idealists from the French revolutionaries, and stimulated by prophetic and divine visions, Blake composed hundreds of pages of dark, cryptic, and often unfathomable poetry and prose, decorated with hundreds of illustrations. His book *The Marriage of Heaven and Hell* is an outstanding demonstration of Blake's unique talents. Writing in the style of the Bible's books of prophecy, Blake provides his own romantic and revolutionary visions in the work.

With titles such as "The Voice of the Devil" and "Proverbs of Hell," Blake paints a vision of hell not as a place where the wicked are punished but as a positive source of primal energy. This belief led Blake to the controversial conclusion that "the road of excess leads to the palace of wisdom."[56] Although this line is often repeated today, when it was written it was considered blasphemous by those who believed

William Blake created handmade books of his poems in which the printed words were entwined with the illustrations. Shown here is the piece "The Little Girl Lost."

JOHN CONSTABLE'S LANDSCAPES

John Constable (1776–1837) was a British romantic artist known for the landscape paintings he made of the region of Suffolk now known as "Constable Country." His biography appears on Olga's Gallery Web site:

John Constable was one of the major European landscape artists of the nineteenth century, whose art was admired by Delacroix and Gericault and influenced the . . . Impressionists, although he did not achieve much fame during his lifetime in England, his own country. John Constable was born in East Bergholt, Suffolk. . . .

In 1796–1798 he took lessons from John Thomas Smith and later from George Frost, who supported his love of landscape painting and encouraged him to study [Thomas] Gainsborough's works. In 1700 he entered the Royal Academy Schools. . . . Though deeply impressed by the . . . watercolors of Thomas Girtin, Constable believed the actual study of nature was more important than any artistic model. He refused to "learn the truth second-hand." To a greater degree than any other artist before him, Constable based his paintings on precisely drawn sketches made directly from nature.

The spectacular sky in John Constable's painting Stonehenge *is meant to impart a feeling of exhilaration and wonder.*

Olga's Gallery, "John Constable," 2006. www.abcgallery.com/c/constable/constablebio.html.

that spiritual knowledge could be attained only through prayer and religious meditation. As Kazin writes, Blake had

> taken on himself the burden of proving that man is an independent spiritual being. This required the refutation of all existing literature. The tortured rhetoric . . . is not a lapse from taste; it is the awful wilderness into which Blake had to enter by the nature of his staggering task. This was to give man a new Bible, and with it a new natural history; a new cosmogony, and with it his own version, supplanting Hebrew and Greek literature, of man's first self-consciousness in the universe. . . . To Blake the myth-maker, the age required a new Bible. . . . [His books] are in fact an attempt to create, on the basis of a private myth, a new epic literature that would ride the currents of the age.[57]

Blake's desire to provide humanity with a new mythology inspired him to produce several major canvases and more than a half-dozen handmade books, including *The Book of Thel, Visions of the Daughters of Albion, America, Europe, The Boot of Urizen, Milton,* and *Jerusalem.* Although few original copies of these dense, esoteric works have survived, they were reproduced in later years and may now be found on the Internet.

These books have inspired generations of artists and writers from Delacroix to twentieth-century singer/songwriter Bob Dylan; however, Blake's brilliance went largely unrecognized in his lifetime. He was considered an eccentric by most and a madman by some. His influence started to grow only after he died in 1827. The Irish romantic poet and mystic W.B. Yeats first read Blake when he was fifteen, and in 1887 he wrote the essay "William Blake and the Imagination," which stimulated a new interest in the romantic poet and painter and elevated his reputation among critics, artists, and the general public.

Light and Landscapes

If Blake had been willing to paint romantic landscapes, he probably would not have had to live in poverty. In the early years of the nineteenth century, landscape painters with Blake's skill were highly celebrated in England. Many of them worked with both watercolors and oil paints. Some were able to amass fortunes by selling engraved prints of their works or by having them reproduced in books with titles such as *Picturesque Views of the Southern Coast of England.*

Many landscapes were accurate representations of fields, forests, cliffs, and seascapes that were created for the viewer's enjoyment or for scientific or historical purposes. By the beginning of the nineteenth century, however, subject matter turned from the objective to the sublime, what Honour refers to as "the exhilarating terror inspired by rushing torrents, roaring waterfalls, precipitous crags, [and] unattainable mountain peaks."[58] Besides terror, the romantic landscape painters sought to impart meaning and symbolism into pictures of sun rays, clouds, rain, shadows, and gloom.

Painting Light

One of the first painters to practice this art was Thomas Girtin, who created dramatic watercolors of ruins, abbeys, and castles. Considered one of the earliest romantic innovators, Girtin was a master at creating powerful contrasts between dark and light areas of a picture.

In typical romantic fashion, Girtin's life was tragically short—he died at the age of twenty-seven. His talents were undeniable, however, allegedly prompting England's most celebrated landscape artist, Joseph Mallord William Turner, to quip, "Had Girtin lived I should have starved."[59] Whether or not this anecdote is true, there is little doubt that the two artists shared a common interest in moonlight, sunlight, and clouds.

Turner, who was born in London in 1775, showed his first major work, *Fishermen at Sea,* in a Royal Academy exhibition in 1796. Even at this early date, Turner used natural illumination as the main subject of the painting. John Piper, commenting on this talent, writes in *British Romantic Artists* that Turner "painted *light*—veiled light, or misty light, or full light, or

blinding light."[60] In *Fishermen at Sea*, spectacular black clouds bend and shape the luminosity in the sky while blotting out the sun. The ostensible subjects of the painting, the fishermen in their boat in the middle of a churning sea, are blurry and insignificant.

Turner's ability to convey the sublime brought him early fame. At the age of twenty-six he was elected to the prestigious position of president of the Royal Academy. In the years that followed, the artist traveled extensively throughout Great Britain and Europe, completing dozens of watercolor and oil paintings of historical scenes, shipwrecks, and disasters. In most, the atmospheric lighting plays a major role.

Turner was also fascinated with the drama of the sea and at one point decided to risk his life in order to get firsthand experience of the storm-tossed ocean: "I got the sailors [on the

Joseph Mallord William Turner was known for expertly depicting natural light, as demonstrated by the dramatic black clouds and veiled moon in *Fishermen at Sea*.

Ariel] to lash me to the mast to observe [the storm]. I was lashed for four hours and did not expect to escape, but I felt bound to record it."[61] The result was a painting with the unusually long title *Snowstorm—steam-boat off a harbour mouth making signals in shallow water, and going by the lead. The Author was in this storm on the night the* Ariel *left Harwich.*

Ironically, while the artist faced death to create the piece, Turner never exhibited *Snowstorm* during his lifetime. Indeed, three-quarters of his many paintings were not put on public display until five decades after his death in 1851. (Astonishingly, in 1939, about fifty unknown Turner canvases were discovered rolled up in the basement of the National Gallery in London. Building managers at first mistook them for dusty old tarpaulins.) Despite the lack of public exposure, however, Turner was able to earn a fortune through sales of prints and books. His work also influenced a score of other important British romantic painters, including John Constable, John Ruskin, John Martin, Edwin Landseer, and John Everett Millais.

Through landscapes, light, and visions past, present, and future, the romantics of Great Britain left their marks on the world of art. And in doing so, they posed questions and presented answers still pondered nearly two centuries later.

Romanticism in the American Wilderness

W hen the romantic movement first developed in Europe, the United States did not officially exist. Yet the majority of Americans at that time could trace their ancestry directly to Great Britain, while a minority were from Germany and France. In addition, several well-known American artists traveled to London and Paris, where they were exposed to the romantic tradition. As a result, by the time the United States was officially created in 1783, there were several American painters, called international romantics, who specialized in the emotional, exotic, dramatic, ancient, or natural themes associated with romantic art.

The international romantics introduced the European style to American artists, and by the 1800s a separate school called native romanticism had developed in the United States. The native artists worked in an environment unlike any found in Europe. During the first half of the nineteenth century, when the movement was in full flower, the North American continent was in a pristine natural state and was principally occupied by Native Americans. Because the bulk of the white population lived along the East Coast, the prairies, mountains, deserts, and forests of western North America were unknown to most Americans, as were the native inhabitants. Pictures painted by artists, often reproduced in books, were the only record of the vast continent. For this reason, American artists were less apt to create works that were overemotional and excessively dramatic. As James Thrall Soby and Dorothy C. Miller explain in *Romantic Painting in America*,

> [Our] early landscapists took their basic inspiration, direct and raw, from the rich wilderness of nature, first in the East and later in the West. . . . The native Romantic artist of 1820–1850 was less the confessor of egocentric emotion than a celebrant of a national landscape and mythology. Though spiritually akin to his European counterpart, he was on the whole far less introspective.[62]

The American Romantics in London

The roots of the romantic movement in the United States can be traced back to the 1770s, when three American artists, Benjamin West from Pennsylvania, John Trumbull from Connecticut, and John Singleton Copley from Boston, worked and studied in London. At that time, the romantic movement was in its infancy, but these American artists created paintings that proved to be innovative and inspirational to European artists. For example, Copley's 1778 painting *Watson and the Shark* is strikingly similar to *Raft of the* Medusa, painted by French romantic Géricault forty-four years later.

Watson and the Shark shows a young man struggling on his back in the sea as a huge shark lunges at him with an open mouth. Nearby, men in a rowboat strain to reach the imperiled man as several oarsmen row forcefully to position the boat. At the prow, a man with a long boat hook attempts to fight off the shark.

Watson and the Shark was inspired by an event that took place in Havana, Cuba, in 1749, when a fourteen-year-old orphan, Brook Watson, was attacked by a shark while swimming in the harbor. Shipmates nearby launched a courageous rescue effort and the boy survived, though the shark tore his leg off below the knee. It is believed that Copley probably met Watson in London around 1774 and later created *Watson and the Shark*. The painting fits into the romantic category by way of its relatively current subject matter and its grisly, sensational depiction of reality.

West's Epic Representation

Copley was mainly a portraitist, and *Watson and the Shark* was his only romantic painting. Benjamin West, however, was at the center of the London romantic movement in the late 1770s. Born in 1738, West studied in Italy, where he adopted the controlled, detailed techniques of neoclassicism. West's

Watson and the Shark by John Singleton Copley shows sailors desperately trying to rescue a young man who is being menaced by an open-mouthed shark.

Benjamin West's *Saul and the Witch of Endor* depicts a biblical scene in eerie and supernatural fashion.

style began to change when he was exposed to Burke's theories on the sublime and the works of William Blake and Henry Fuseli. Wishing to keep up with the times, the American artist began painting supernatural and fantastic re-creations of scenes from Shakespeare, medieval Gothic history, and the Bible. One of the earliest paintings of this type, which the painter called epic representation, was the eerie *Saul and the Witch of Endor*. According to Soby and Miller, this painting of a biblical scene "typifies Romanticism of the supernatural and the wild, which . . . was to receive new impetus from the 'Gothick' tales of English and German novelists in the late 18th century and was finally to become a recurrent preoccupation among 19th century Romantic artists."[63]

In 1817, West's interest in romanticism reached its zenith in the large-scale painting *Death on the Pale Horse*, a scene taken from a sketch the artist had created in 1802. The story of the pale horse is from the Book of Revelation: "And I looked, and behold, a pale horse: and his name that sat on him was Death, and Hell followed with him."[64] Created when the artist was seventy-nine, the enormous canvas, 15 by 26 feet (4.5 by 8m), portrays a scene in sensationalized romantic style. Figures gesticulate in melodramatic fashion as they flail against death, falling and fighting while cloaked in resplendent light and shadowy darkness.

Romantics in America

West, who served as president of the prestigious Royal Academy from 1792 until his death in 1820, received many commissions from King George III and other English aristocrats. The painter was also known for his compassion toward art students, and he acted as teacher and mentor to three generations of American artists in London. One of West's pupils at the Royal Academy, Washington Allston, brought the skills he learned in London back to the United States in 1818.

Allston, born in South Carolina in 1779, was both a painter and a poet. Like many romantics, he was entranced by the morbid, lonely, and morose drama of the English Gothic style. Allston stated that he developed an early love of the "wild and marvelous" countryside of South Carolina and also "delighted in being terrified by the tales of witches and hags, which the Negroes used to tell me."[65]

Allston was an avid reader and about one-third of the nearly two hundred paintings he made during his career are based on the Bible or literature by Shakespeare, Milton, Coleridge, Walter Scott, or Washington Irving. This fascination with the written word lay at the heart of Allston's artistic philosophy. According to Abraham A. Davidson, in *The Eccentrics and Other American Visionary Painters*, "Allston urged that the artist read as extensively and as persistently as the

THOUGHTS WRITTEN ON A WALL

Washington Allston was both a productive painter and a prolific writer who often scribbled his thoughts on his studio wall. In his book Lectures on Art, *Allston published more than forty aphorisms, excerpted below from the Project Gutenberg Web site:*

If an Artist love his Art for its own sake, he will delight in excellence wherever he meets it, as well in the work of another as in his own. This is the test of a true love. . . .

Distinction is the consequence, never the object, of a great mind.

The love of gain never made a Painter; but it has marred many . . . .

Selfishness in Art, as in other things, is sensibility kept at home. . . .

The most intangible, and therefore the worst, kind of lie is a half truth. . . .

No right judgment can ever be formed on any subject having a moral or intellectual bearing without benevolence; for so strong is man's natural self-bias, that, without this restraining principle, he insensibly becomes a competitor in all such cases presented to his mind…. In other words, no one can see any thing as it really is through the misty spectacles of self-love. . . . Never, therefore, expect justice from a vain man.

Washington Allston, "Lectures on Art," Project Gutenberg, March 1, 2004. www.gutenberg.org/files/11391/11391-h/11391-h.htm#ch01.

poet. His own private library must have been one of the most impressive in America."[66]

Through his research, Allston came to believe that artists should not attempt to re-create a strictly pictorial view of a scene. Instead, they should use the details of a story to stimulate the imagination in order to create a grand canvas. For example, many artists re-created literal scenes from the Bible to provide moral instruction. Allston, however, used the Bible and other books as a springboard for his creativity. In order to fuel his imagination, the painter meditated on a tale, read between the lines, looked at it from several different points of view, and then set his brush to canvas in a rush of inspiration. The result was often a sensationalized canvas that astounded the viewer.

The painting *Moonlit Landscape*, created in 1819, is typical of Allston's quintessentially romantic style. Although the moon shines brightly in the center of the canvas, the shadowy lighting is more characteristic of a setting sun than a rising moon. Mountains, trees, a river, and a bridge are depicted in a dreamlike haze while four small, insignificant figures stand in the foreground. There is more to this simple scene than meets the eye, according to Davidson, who explains its romantic symbolism:

> The intrusion of the tiny shadowy figures—a group of three who have stopped to speak with a horseman— lend an air of brooding mystery to the silent nightscape. At the same time, the slow movement of the serrated clouds about to cover the moon . . . hints at the potential for change, even violence, within the now stationary figures.[67]

Allston painted other works that helped define American romanticism, including *Diana and Her Nymphs in the Chase*, *Ships at Sea*, and *Rise of a Thunderstorm at Sea*, but the artist's greatest vision was also his most tortured work. The painter labored on the 12 by 16 foot (3.6 x 4.8m) canvas *Belshazzar's Feast* from 1817 until his death in 1843. During these twenty-six years, the perfectionist Allston repainted the scene countless times, beginning with a nearly finished work in 1818 and ending with an unfinished canvas that was nearly blank.

The work occupied such a large part of Allston's life that the painter's death was seen as a relief to his friend R.H. Dana, who wrote: "[Upon Allston's death he] had escaped that terrible vision—the nightmare, the incubus, the tormentor of his life—his unfinished picture."[68] This comment is all the more surprising because Allston often worked very quickly, finishing some paintings in as little as three weeks.

The Hudson River School

Allston's uncompleted canvas kept him mostly home in Cambridgeport, Massachusetts, during the last years of his life. By contrast, several other American romantics spent their days traipsing through New York's Hudson River Valley, the Catskill and Adirondack mountains, and the White Mountains in New Hampshire. During this era, these densely forested mountains, sparsely populated and pristine, inspired the romantics to develop their own specific style of painting, called the Hudson River School. (In this usage, the word *school* does not refer to a learning institution but is used to define a group of people who share a similar artistic philosophy and style.)

The founder of the Hudson River School was Thomas Cole, a native of England born in 1801 who moved to New York City when he was nineteen years old. In 1825, Cole made his first journey up the Hudson River, where he painted three landscapes. Upon returning to the city, Cole tried to sell his paintings by placing them in the window of a bookstore. They were seen by celebrated artist John Trumbull, who had won fame for the many paintings he had made of scenes from the Revolutionary War, including *The Declaration of Independence* and *The Surrender of General Burgoyne at Saratoga*, which now hang in the United States Capitol. Trumbull bought one of Cole's canvases and introduced the young painter to some wealthy friends, who quickly became his patrons.

In the years that followed the sale of his first paintings, Cole became one of the most renowned painters in the United States. His work combined strikingly inspirational pictures of mountains, streams, and woodlands with a touch of the fantastical.

The Giant's Chalice, painted in 1833, is a good example of Cole's deft touch when blending the natural with the supernatural into a romantic masterpiece. The canvas is described by Wolf:

> Prompted by the picture's title, one might well imagine oneself gazing with a giant's eyes over an infinite expanse of mountains, high plateaus, and ocean bays that diminishes into the distance and virtually continues beyond the picture edges, with a seaside town lost, like a tiny anthill, in the grandiose wilderness panorama. The compositional structure might recall earlier universal landscapes, were it not for a disturbing factor. On a rocky plateau projecting into the picture . . . rises a huge stone chalice [goblet] whose shaft consists of a gigantic primordial tree and whose base and rim are overgrown with forests interspersed with ancient settlements. The chalice is filled with water that serves tiny sailboats as a landlocked sea.[69]

Washington Allston's *Elijah in the Desert* reveals the artist's fascination with the desolate and morbid elements of romantic art.

The subject matter of *The Giant's Chalice* was derived from Cole's belief that the American landscape, in its pristine state, was so grand that it might once have been inhabited by a race of giants, now mysteriously extinct. The current small inhabitants, because of their limited view, cannot perceive the giant's drinking cup, but instead sail their boats upon it and build their homes below it, unaware of the grandeur before their eyes.

Cole's commentary on a modern society blind to the earth's wonders had ties to the painter's visits to Europe, where he observed a natural landscape tamed and subservient to society's demands. Writing for *American Monthly Magazine* in 1836, the artist described his view of Europe: "The primitive features of the scenery have long since been destroyed or modified—the extensive forests that once overshadowed a great part of it have been felled—rugged mountains have been smoothed, and impetuous rivers turned from their courses to accommodate the tastes and necessities of a dense population."[70]

Thomas Cole used romantic elements to express his awe of nature in paintings such as *View from Mount Holyoke,* widely considered a masterpiece of American landscape painting.

Cole's reverence for nature was obvious in the dozens of paintings he created before his death in 1848. The works combine many typical features of romanticism, including strong contrasts between light and dark, insignificant people beneath moody or remarkable clouds, and supernatural worlds both fantastic and phantasmagoric. Unlike European romantics, however, Cole did not often have to stray far from reality to portray a natural paradise. All he had to do was to paint what he saw outside the window of his Catskill home and add a startlingly contrasting element, such as a castle in the sky, a giant's drinking cup, or a ghostly fairy on a riverbank.

Frederic Church: An Abiding Sense of Awe

Cole inspired a number of painters who worked between 1855 and 1875, including Asher Brown Durand, John Quidor, and Sanford Robinson Gifford. The only painter to rival Cole in success, however, was Frederic Edwin Church, who dominated the second generation of artists in the Hudson River School.

Church was born into a family of great wealth in 1826 and became a pupil of Cole's at age eighteen. In the years that followed, Church spent every year from spring to autumn walking through the wilderness of New York State, making sketches. In the winter, he returned to his studio to create and sell paintings.

Later in his career Church traveled to exotic locations, such as northern Labrador in Canada, where he made huge canvases of ice fields and icebergs. After visiting South America, Church created one of his most colossal paintings, *The Heart of the Andes*, on a 5 by 10 foot (1.5 by 3m) canvas. When the artist exhibited the painting in 1859, he did so in a fashion that German romantic painter Philipp Otto Runge described as total art. *The Heart of the Andes* was installed in a darkened chamber, where it was moodily illuminated by gas jets concealed behind silver reflectors. The surrounding walls were decorated with specially designed curtains and hung with palm fronds that were meant to create an exotic atmosphere for viewers.

Church's innovative exhibition created a public sensation, and each month twelve to thirteen thousand people paid twenty-five cents apiece to file by the painting. Eventually *The Heart of the Andes* was sold for ten thousand dollars, the highest price ever paid for a work by a living American artist at that time. On the Web Gallery of Art, Emil Kren and Daniel Marx explain why the work was so admired:

> Church painted nature with uncanny fidelity and an abiding sense of awe. His landscapes embodied America's belief that the opening of frontiers and territorial expansion were the nation's destiny. . . . In many ways, the painting carried the ideas of the Hudson River School to their most dramatic culmination.[71]

Romantic Art in the American West

In the decades between Thomas Cole's first paintings in the 1820s and Church's exhibition in the late 1850s, the population of New York more than doubled. As the forests fell and the countryside filled with farmhouses and towns, Americans traveled west in increasing numbers. By the end of the nineteenth century, the United States was settled from the Atlantic to the Pacific. During the so-called taming of the American West, tens of thousands of Native Americans were pushed off their ancestral lands and exiled to reservations. Even as this forced migration was happening, the lives of the indigenous peoples were romanticized by artists who viewed American Indians as exotic "noble savages."

The first romantic artist to travel west of the Appalachian Mountains was George Catlin, who was a scientist as well as a painter. Beginning in 1830, Catlin spent eight years traveling thousands of miles back and forth between the American West and the East Coast. During his travels from present-day Oklahoma to the Dakotas, he visited about fifty Indian tribes and painted over five hundred landscapes, scenes of tribal villages, and portraits.

JOHN QUIDOR'S ROMANTIC HORRORS

Unlike their European counterparts most American romantics avoided depictions of the shocking and bizarre. One exception was John Quidor, as James Thrall Soby and Dorothy C. Miller explain in Romantic Painting in America:

John Quidor, born in 1801 . . . was almost unknown to his contemporaries and exerted little or no influence over the art of his period. His earliest known painting, dated 1823, was of a scene from *Don Quixote*, and he subsequently took a majority of his subjects from literature, particularly from that of his countrymen, Washington Irving and James Fenimore Cooper.

Quidor's *Ichabod Crane Pursued by the Headless Horseman of Sleepy Hollow,* was exhibited in 1828 and inaugurated a career devoted to horror Romanticism—a depiction of witchery, dark legend and terror—which if anything intensified the macabre humor of its literary sources. . . . In many of his canvases nature is . . . a conniving and active agent in [outlaw] activity. . . . In *The Money Diggers* the foreground figure and tree are nearly identical in pose and intent, while the remainder of the landscape writhes with its own sinister activity. For Quidor man and nature were related in evil far more intimately than Cole had attempted to relate them for good.

James Thrall Soby and Dorothy C. Miller, *Romantic Painting in America*. New York: Museum of Modern Art, 1969, p. 21.

Although Catlin thought of the Native Americans as primitives, he was enthralled by their physiques, which he compared to figures immortalized in ancient Greek sculpture. Catlin was also alarmed by the encroachment of whites on Indian lands and embraced the romantic notion that his paintings could motivate society to preserve what was quickly becoming a vanishing way of life. A Smithsonian Institution Web page explains:

> When Catlin first traveled west in 1830, the United States Congress had just passed the Indian Removal Act, requiring Indians in the Southeast to resettle west of the Mississippi River. This vast forced migration— as well as smallpox epidemics and continuing incursions from trappers, miners, explorers, and settlers— created pressures on Indian cultures to adapt or perish. Seeing the devastation of many tribes, Catlin came to regard the frontier as a region of corruption. He portrayed the nobility of these still-sovereign peoples, but he was aware that he painted in sovereignty's twilight.[72]

George Catlin traveled thousands of miles throughout the West, portraying Native Americans and their ceremonies in works such as *The Bear Dance.*

Catlin began his first journey west along the Missouri River in present-day Kansas, creating landscape paintings such as *River Bluffs, 1320 Miles Above St. Louis*, that showed the West in its natural state. Catlin also idealized his subjects in portraits such as *La-dóo-ke-a, Buffalo Bull, a Grand Pawnee Warrior*, which shows a Pawnee warrior in ceremonial dress. Paintings such as *Buffalo Hunt under the Wolf-skin Mask* were

meant to educate the public about traditional Native American hunting techniques.

During the late 1830s and 1840s, Catlin traveled throughout eastern America and Europe, hoping to publicize the plight of the Native Americans. Like many romantic artists, however, he found few who were interested in his life's work, and he went bankrupt in 1852. A wealthy patron obtained Catlin's paintings after his death in 1872 and donated them to the Smithsonian Institution in Washington, D.C. Today those romantic landscapes and portraits, according to the Smithsonian Web site, are "recognized as a great cultural treasure, offering rare insight into native cultures and a crucial chapter in American history."[73]

Catlin was one of several romantic painters whose work provides a historic account of the native inhabitants of the American West. Others, such as George Caleb Bingham, recorded another chapter, that of white trappers and explorers. Bingham's paintings, such as *Fur Traders Descending the Missouri* and *Daniel Boone Escorting a Band of Pioneers into the Western Country*, romanticize the American pioneer spirit that helped define the nation in the nineteenth century. Another romantic painter, Albert Bierstadt, created stunning romantic landscapes such as *Half Dome, Yosemite* and *Storm in the Rocky Mountains*, providing a romantic vision of the fascinating natural wonders found in the far West.

A Bygone Age

By the 1880s, the romantic movement was all but dead in Europe, replaced by realism, a school of art that valued natural representations of people, places, and things; however, romanticism continued to grow and evolve in the United States. In the 1890s painters such as Albert Pinkham Ryder developed a style called high romanticism, which embraced all the most sensationalized elements of early European romantics. For example, Ryder's paintings *Siegfried and the Rhine Maidens* and *The Race Track (Death on a Pale Horse)* recall works by Fuseli and Blake.

The eerie *The Race Track (Death on a Pale Horse)* by Albert Pinkham Ryder features some of the most sensational aspects of early European romanticism.

Ryder, like Blake, was an eccentric who considered himself a mystic. According to biographer Frederic Sherman, the artist "was exalted, solitary, living in constant and fierce communion with his own inner world of imagination, awaiting inspiration as the faithful await miracles and forcing it to its ultimate expression through a figurative prayer and fasting."[74]

Ryder was part of an American romantic tradition that followed its own course, much as the nation did, during the period between the 1770s and the 1900s. From the Revolutionary War to the automobile era, artists recorded not only their creative visions but rapidly passing moments in American history. Those interested in viewing the lost past as seen through the eyes of the nation's greatest artists need only search the Internet for the works of Cole, Church, Catlin, and Ryder. In the brushstrokes these men left on canvas, the past is preserved, along with the ideals of a bygone age.

Notes

Introduction: An Artistic Movement

1. Frederick Cummings, *Romantic Art in Britain*. Philadelphia: Philadelphia Museum of Art, 1968, pp. 17–18.

Chapter 1: Romance and Revolution

2. Lorenz Eitner, ed., *Neoclassicism and Romanticism, 1750–1850*. Englewood Cliffs, NJ: Prentice Hall, 1970, p. 4.
3. Quoted in William Vaughn, *Romanticism and Art*. London: Thames and Hudson, 1994, p. 13.
4. Quoted in Eitner, *Neoclassicism and Romanticism*, pp. 12–13.
5. Petra ten-Doesschate Chu, *Nineteenth Century Art*. New York: Harry N. Abrams, 2003, p. 157.
6. Vaughn, *Romanticism and Art*, pp. 32–33.
7. Vaughn, *Romanticism and Art*, p. 33.
8. Raffaella Russo, *Friedrich*. New York: DK Publishing, 1999, p. 72.
9. Vaughn, *Romanticism and Art*, p. 55.
10. Kenneth Clark, *The Romantic Rebellion*. New York: Harper and Row, 1973, p. 75.
11. Quoted in Chu, *Nineteenth Century Art*, p. 149.
12. Quoted in Chu, *Nineteenth Century Art*, p. 148.
13. Chu, *Nineteenth Century Art*, p. 151.
14. Quoted in Kenneth Clark, "Goya, Francisco," The Artchive, www.artchive.com/artchive/g/goya/may_3rd.jpg.html.
15. Chu, *Nineteenth Century Art*, p. 153.
16. Kathryn Calley Galitz, "Romanticism," Metropolitan Museum of Art, 2006. www.metmuseum.org/toah/hd/roma/hd_roma.htm.

Chapter 2: The German Roots of Romanticism

17. Quoted in Hugh Honour, *Romanticism*. New York: Harper and Row, 1979, p. 219.
18. Honour, *Romanticism*, p. 218.
19. William Vaughn, *German Romantic Painting*. New Haven, CT: Yale University Press, 1980, p. 28.
20. David Jay Brown and Rebecca McClen Novick, "Romanticism," Levity.com, 1997. www.levity.com/mavericks/romantic.htm.
21. Quoted in Eitner, *Neoclassicism and Romanticism*, pp. 76–77.
22. Chu, *Nineteenth Century Art*, p. 158.
23. Quoted in Russo, *Friedrich*, p. 22.
24. Quoted in Vaughn, *German Romantic Painting*, pp. 7–8.
25. Norbert Wolf, *Painting of the Romantic Era*. Cologne, Germany: Tasschen, 1999, p. 43.
26. Quoted in Wolf, *Painting of the Romantic Era*, p. 36.

27. Quoted in Eitner, *Neoclassicism and Romanticism*, p. 146.
28. Quoted in Vaughn, *German Romantic Painting*, p. 57.
29. Quoted in Eitner, *Neoclassicism and Romanticism*, p. 147.
30. Quoted in Vaughn, *German Romantic Painting*, p. 127.
31. Wolf, *Painting of the Romantic Era*, p. 48.

Chapter 3: Politics and Romance in France

32. Clark, *Romantic Rebellion*, p. 36.
33. Vaughn, *Romanticism and Art*, p. 62.
34. Clark, *Romantic Rebellion*, p. 178.
35. Quoted in Chu, *Nineteenth Century Art*, p. 199.
36. Quoted in Chu, *Nineteenth Century Art*, p. 200.
37. Chu, *Nineteenth Century Art*, p. 201.
38. Quoted in The Getty, "Théodore Géricault," 2006. www.getty.edu/art/gettyguide/artmakerdetails?maker=498&page=1.
39. Honour, *Romanticism*, p. 41.
40. Vaughn, *Romanticism and Art*, p. 244.
41. Quoted in Vaughn, *Romanticism and Art*, p. 244.
42. Wolf, *Painting of the Romantic Era*, p. 105.
43. Quoted in Chu, *Nineteenth Century Art*, p. 211.
44. Chu, *Nineteenth Century Art*, p. 213.

Chapter 4: A Different Type of Revolution in Great Britain

45. Graham Hough, *The Last Romantics*. New York: University Paperbacks, 1961, p. xi.
46. Cummings, *Romantic Art in Britain*, p. 17.
47. Cummings, *Romantic Art in Britain*, p. 18.
48. Horace Walpole, "Reviews of *The Castle of Otranto* by Horace Walpole," Project Gutenberg, August 12, 2005. www.gutenberg.org/catalog/world/reviews?fk_books=696.
49. Keith Parkins, "Horace Walpole," Keith Parkins' Home Page, June 1999. www.heureka.clara.net/art/walpole.htm.
50. Cummings, *Romantic Art in Britain*, p. 71.
51. Cummings, *Romantic Art in Britain*, p. 173.
52. Quoted in John Piper, *British Romantic Artists*. London: Collins, 1946, p. 26.
53. Chu, *Nineteenth Century Art*, p. 79.
54. Alfred Kazin, "An Introduction to William Blake," Multimedia Library, 2006. www.multimedialibrary.com/articles/kazin/alfredblake.asp.
55. William Blake, "Songs of Innocence and Songs of Experience," Project Gutenberg, March 28, 2003. www.gutenberg.org/dirs/etext99/sinex10h.htm#43.
56. William Blake, "The Marriage of Heaven and Hell," Alchemy Web Site, 2006. www.levity.com/alchemy/blake_ma.html.
57. Kazin, "An Introduction to William Blake."
58. Honour, *Romanticism*, pp. 57–58.
59. Quoted in Piper, *British Romantic Artists*, p. 16.
60. Piper, *British Romantic Artists*, p. 17.
61. Quoted in Clark, *Romantic Rebellion*, p. 243.

Chapter 5: Romanticism in the American Wilderness

62. James Thrall Soby and Dorothy C. Miller, *Romantic Painting in America*. New York: Museum of Modern Art, 1969, p. 8.

63. Soby and Miller, *Romantic Painting in America*, p. 10.

64. Rev. 6:8.

65. Quoted in Soby and Miller, *Romantic Painting in America*, p. 11.

66. Davidson, *Eccentrics and Other American Visionary Painters*, p. 10.

67. Davidson, *Eccentrics and Other American Visionary Painters*, p. 12.

68. Quoted in Jared B. Flagg, *The Life and Letters of Washington Allston.* New York: Charles Scribner's Sons, 1892, p. 333.

69. Wolf, *Painting of the Romantic Era*, p. 127.

70. Quoted in John W. McCourbrey, *American Art, 1700–1960: Sources and Documents.* Englewood Cliffs, NJ: Prentice Hall, 1965, p. 102.

71. Emil Kren and Daniel Marx, "The Heart of the Andes," Web Gallery of Art, 2006. www.wga.hu/frames-e.html?/html/c/church/heartande.html.

72. Smithsonian American Art Museum, "Catlin Virtual Exhibition." 2006. http://americanart.si.edu/collections/exhibits/catlin/highlights.html.

73. Smithsonian American Art Museum, "Catlin Virtual Exhibition."

74. Frederic Fairchild Sherman, *Albert Pinkham Ryder.* New York: privately printed, no date, p. 38.

For Further Reading

Books

Rosie Dickins, *The Usborne Introduction to Art: In Association with the National Gallery, London*. Tulsa: EDC Publishing, 2004. Detailed introduction to the history of art with Internet links about featured artists and examples of their work and works by related artists.

John M. Dunn, *The French Revolution: The Fall of the Monarchy*. Farmington Hills, MI: Gale, 2003. Describes how the French Revolution replaced old social rules and regulations with new laws and methods of government.

Sarah Halliwell, ed., *The Romantics*. Austin, TX: Raintree Steck-Vaughn, 1998. Introduces some of the major artists, writers, and composers who flourished in Europe and the United States during the Romantic era in the late eighteenth and early nineteenth centuries.

Don Nardo, *Ancient Greece*. Farmington Hills, MI: Lucent Books, 2006. The history of ancient Greece, including a chapter on society and culture during the Classical period.

Mike Venezia, *Eugène Delecroix*. New York: Children's Press, 2003. Describes the life and career of the nineteenth-century French Romantic artist Eugène Delacroix, whose experiments with color and scenes of action led to Impressionism and other modern art styles.

Patricia Wright, *Goya*. New York: Dorling Kindersley, 2000. The story of the tormented Romantic painter Francisco Goya, with dozens of color illustrations and drawings.

Web Sites

The Artchive (http://artchive.com). An online art gallery with scans of more than two thousand paintings by two hundred artists as well as art reviews, theory and criticism, and exhibitions by Goya and others.

National Gallery of Art (www.nga.gov/onlinetours/index.shtm). This Web site, run by the National Gallery of Art in Washington, D.C., features artist biographies along with hundreds of pages of paintings, photographs, and sculptures, some available for viewing via virtual reality gallery tours.

Olga's Gallery (www.abcgallery.com). An online art museum with a comprehensive collection containing more than ten thousand full-color works of art, artist biographies, and other information concerning painters and paintings.

Web Gallery of Art (www.wga.hu/welcome.html). The Web Gallery of Art is a virtual museum and searchable database of European and American painting and sculpture from the twelfth to the mid-nineteenth century, including a nice selection of Romantic artists.

The William Blake Page (www.gailgastfield.com/blake.html). Reproductions of the art and poems of the revered Romantic William Blake, taken from his exceptional handmade books.

Index

(Géricault), 54–58
Ramdohr, Freiherr von, 35
rational thought, 8, 14, 44
realism, 48, 93
redemption, 36
Reign of Terror, 44, 45, 73
religious elation, 31, 38
Restoration period, 48–61
revolution
    artistic reactions to, 10, 20,
        22, 51–52
    Enlightenment thought
        and, 14
    French Revolution, 20, 22,
        44, 45, 72–73
    heroic style and, 46
    romanticism as reaction to,
        13–27
Reynolds, Joshua, 15, 17
Robespierre, Maximilien de,
    45, 46
Romance of the Forest
    (Radcliffe), 67
Romantic Art in Britain
    (Cummings), 11–12
romantic artists
    criticism of, 17
    innovations of, 8–10
    inspirations for, 18–19
    reactions of, to war and rev-
        olution, 10, 20, 22, 51–52
    self-expression by, 12, 13
    see also specific artists
romantic imagination, 15, 17
romanticism
    in America, 79–94
    in Britain, 62–78
    decline of, 93–94
    in France, 44–61
    in Germany, 28–43
    influence of, 12
    as new attitude, 17–18
    public acceptance of, 49
    public interest in, 12
    revolution and, 13–27
Romanticism and Art
    (Vaughn), 17, 18, 47

Romantic Painting in America
    (Soby and Miller), 80
romantic poetry, 19, 21
Romantic Rebellion, The
    (Clark), 23
Rottman, Carl, 43
Royal Academy, 83
Runge, Philipp Otto, 37–40,
    89
Russo, Raffaella, 19–20
Ryder, Albert Pinkham,
    93–94

Salon, 49–50, 52, 58
Saturn Devouring His Son
    (Goya), 26
Saul and the Witch of Endor
    (West), 82
Schinkel, Karl Friedrich, 43
sculptures, Greek, 15
self-expression, 12, 13
Shakespeare, William, 71
Shelley, Mary, 19, 67
Shelley, Percy Bysshe, 19, 21
Sherman, Frederic, 94
Snowstorm (Turner), 78
Soby, James Thrall, 80
Songs of Experience (Blake),
    71–72
Songs of Innocence (Blake),
    71–72
Sorrows of Young Werther, The
    (Goethe), 31
spirituality, expressed in land-
    scapes, 35
Staël, Germaine de, 49–50, 51
*Starry Sky for the Queen of
    Night* (Schinkel), 43
Stendhal, 50
Storm and Stress movement,
    29, 31
Strasbourg Cathedral, 19
Stubbs, George, 65, 67–68
Sturm and Drang movement,
    29, 31
sublime, 17–18
    depiction of, 26–27, 68–71,

76–78
    in landscapes, 26–27, 76–78
suffering, exploration of,
    53–58
supernatural images, 18–19,
    82, 87
symbols
    of death, 19–20
    see also images

theatrical sets, 43
total art, 39–40, 46, 89
traditions, rebellion against, 8
Trumbull, John, 80, 86
Turner, Joseph Mallord
    William, 10, 76–78

United States. *See* American
    romanticism
utopia, 14

Vaughn, William, 17, 18, 22,
    29, 47, 57–58
Vernet, Horace, 50–53
View from Mount Holyoke
    (Cole), 88
Voltaire, 44

Walpole, Horace, 66, 67–68
war
    artistic reactions to, 20, 22,
        24–26
    depictions of, 52–53
    horrors of, 48
    see also revolution
Watson and the Shark
    (Copley), 80–81
West, Benjamin, 80, 81–83
wilderness, idealization of, 10
Winckelmann, Johann
    Joachim, 15–16, 29
wizards, 18–19
Wolf, Norbert, 36
Wordsworth, William, 19
Wright, Joseph, 68

Yeats, W.B., 75

Picture Credits

About the Author

Stuart A. Kallen is the author of more than two hundred nonfiction books for children and young adults. He has written on topics ranging from the theory of relativity to the history of rock and roll. In addition, Mr. Kallen has written award-winning children's videos and television scripts. In his spare time, Stuart A. Kallen is a singer/songwriter/guitarist in San Diego, California.